A Canterbury Pilgrimage

An Italian Pilgrimage

# A Canterbury Pilgrimage

ELIZABETH ROBINS PENNELL & JOSEPH PENNELL

# An Italian Pilgrimage

*Edited and with an Introduction by Dave Buchanan*

THE UNIVERSITY
*of* ALBERTA PRESS

Published by
The University of Alberta Press
Ring House 2
Edmonton, Alberta, Canada T6G 2E1
www.uap.ualberta.ca

**Library and Archives Canada**
**Cataloguing in Publication**
Pennell, Elizabeth Robins, 1855–1936, author,
illustrator
    A Canterbury pilgrimage/An Italian
pilgrimage / Elizabeth Robins Pennell
& Joseph Pennell ; edited and with an
introduction by Dave Buchanan.

(Wayfarer series)
Contains reprint of A Canterbury pilgrimage
and An Italian pilgrimage.
Includes bibliographical references and index.
Issued in print and electronic formats.
ISBN 978–1–77212–042–4 (paperback).—
ISBN 978–1–77212–092–9 (epub).—
ISBN 978–1–77212–093–6 (kindle).—
ISBN 978–1–77212–094–3 (pdf)

        1. Pennell, Joseph, 1857–1926—
Travel—England. 2. Pennell, Joseph,
1857–1926—Travel—Italy. 3. Pennell,
Elizabeth Robins, 1855–1936—Travel—
England. 4. Pennell, Elizabeth Robins,
1855–1936—Travel—Italy. 5. Bicycle
touring—England. 6. Bicycle touring—
Italy. 7. England—Description and travel.
8. Italy—Description and travel. I. Pennell,
Joseph, 1857–1926, author, illustrator
II. Buchanan, Dave, 1967–, editor III.
Pennell, Joseph, 1857–1926. Italian
pilgrimage IV. Pennell, Joseph, 1857–1926.
Canterbury pilgrimage V. Title.
VI. Title: Italian pilgrimage. VII. Series:
Wayfarer series (Edmonton, Alta.)

DA625.P45 2015          914.204'81
C2015-906271-3
C2015-906272-1

Index available in print and PDF editions.

First edition, first printing, 2015.
Printed and bound in Canada by Houghton
Boston printers, Saskatoon, Saskatchewan.
Copyediting and proofreading by
Brendan Wild.
Indexing by Adrian Mather.

The University of Alberta Press is committed
to protecting our natural environment.
As part of our efforts, this book is printed
on Enviro Paper: it contains 100%
post-consumer recycled fibres and is
acid- and chlorine-free.

The University of Alberta Press gratefully
acknowledges the support received for its
publishing program from the Government of
Canada, the Canada Council for the Arts, and
the Government of Alberta through the Alberta
Media Fund.

Government          Gouvernement
of Canada           du Canada

Canada Council      Conseil des Arts
for the Arts        du Canada

Government

*In memory of Karen Virag, who loved books, travel, and her bicycle*

# Contents

# Acknowledgements

CHAPEAU TO EVERYONE who has engaged in conversation with me about the Pennells over the years, especially Isobel Grundy, Ted Bishop, Glen Norcliffe, Jan Schroeder, Paul Lumsden, Jack Skeffington, David Grant, Bruce Watson, Carol Bell, Bob Povaschuk, Gil Morgan, Cas Horatio, and Victoria Day.

A special thank you to the following: MacEwan University for providing funding for research travel and a sabbatical leave that allowed me time to work on putting together this edition; the interlibrary loan department at MacEwan University Library; the participants at the International Cycling History Conference who keep cycling history alive and who helped inspire this project; the staff at the University of Alberta Press; Lorne Shields for sharing his collection of cycling images; the Victoria and Albert Museum for permission to use the photograph of Elizabeth Robins Pennell; Gerry Hill and Brendan Wild for their keen editorial eyes; and Theresa Agnew, *miri kamli*, my tandem partner on the best adventures.

# Introduction

ONE DAY IN AUGUST 1886, the illustrator and cycling enthusiast Joseph Pennell fell into conversation with two keen "cyclers" in a tavern in Yorkshire, England. The two local wheelmen informed the stranger that an article about tricycling in Italy had appeared recently in *The English Illustrated*.[1] It was written and illustrated, they explained, by "those Pennells"—the well-known American illustrator who "went around with his wife or his sister or *something* all over creation." Joseph played along and never did fess up to the "cyclers" that he was, in fact, one half of those very Pennells. In a letter to his wife and artistic collaborator, the writer Elizabeth Robins Pennell, recounting the incident, Joseph wrote, "Now that [reaction to their work] is better than all the critic stuff" (*Life and Letters of Joseph Pennell*, vol. 1: 181).[2]

This anecdote speaks to the minor celebrity enjoyed in the mid-1880s by this unconventional, creative duo from Philadelphia, who relocated to London in 1884 and embarked on an ambitious series of work-and-play adventures "all over creation"—in England and Europe anyway. They would go on to publish five illustrated cycle-travel books and dozens of illustrated magazine articles about cycling over the next twenty years, in addition to numerous other writing and illustration projects about non-cycling subjects.[3] The Pennells as an artistic team, with her writing and him illustrating (and writing some too), produced some of the earliest and best cycle-travel writing in the early decades of the cycling age and, in the process, helped invent the idea of leisure cycle-touring. But their work and contribution to early cycling culture has been long forgotten by all but a handful of cycling historians.

The Pennells on their tandem Humber tricycle in Perugia, Italy.
Joseph's illustration from *An Italian Pilgrimage*. The machine actually featured
four wheels, counting the small "tipping wheel" at the front. Both riders pedalled.
Luggage was attached to a rack above the rear wheel.

When "those Pennells" are remembered at all today, it is usually for other endeavours. Joseph is known now chiefly as one of America's finest and most prolific illustrators during the great age of American illustration, the period between 1880 and 1910. During these decades, Pennell was "associated with the most important art exhibitions and movements of his day" (*LL1*: vii) and his work filled the pages of popular periodicals in the United States (such as *The Century Magazine and Harper's Monthly*), and England (for instance, *The Illustrated London News* and *St. Nicholas magazine*). His art was featured in countless books authored by some of the finest writers of the era (William Dean Howells, Henry James, Washington Irving).[4] The art historian Joseph Jackson described Pennell as "the greatest American etcher of his time, and one of the leading etchers of all time, but more than that he was a master of pen and ink drawing, and his illustrations for...books remain the best work in the medium we have" (qtd. in Egbert, title page). In particular, Pennell had "a genius for conveying the picturesque" (*LL1*: 55), as his wife put it, urban architecture as well as rural landscapes, first in America, and then abroad, in England and Europe. Henry James, with whom Pennell collaborated on numerous projects, once said that if James's own writing "could ever be what he sometimes dreamed it was, he would give it all up to be able to draw like Pennell" (qtd. in *LL1*: 206).

In addition to being an acclaimed artist, Joseph also wrote extensively about art in works such as *Pen Drawing and Pen Draughtsmen* (1889) and *Lithography and Lithographers* (1898). But Joseph is best remembered for his connection to a much more famous American artist, James McNeill Whistler. The Pennells were close friends with Whistler in London, and together Elizabeth and Joseph wrote one of the first comprehensive biographies of the painter, published in 1908. Later, the Pennells donated their vast collection of Whistleriana to the Library of Congress.[5]

Elizabeth, meanwhile, is known now mostly for her biographies,[6] her art criticism, and her highly original food writing. In fact, her collection of food essays, *The Delights of Delicate Eating*, first published 1896,[7] is still in print. (Her extraordinary collection of Renaissance and eighteenth-century cookbooks was also bequeathed to the Library of Congress.)[8] In recent years, a handful of mostly feminist academics has begun to re-discover and reconsider her contributions as art critic and food writer in the late Victorian period.[9]

Apart from their considerable literary and artistic output, the Pennells were also well connected socially to the literary, intellectual, and visual art scenes in London in the 1880s and 1890s. They hobnobbed regularly with the likes of Edmund Gosse, Oscar Wilde, Bram Stoker, Henry James, J.M.M. Barrie, George Bernard Shaw, and Aubrey Beardsley. Joseph had a reputation as notoriously candid, outspoken, and opinionated. He could be "explosively and injudiciously frank," especially when it came to art, a quality that made him entertaining, if not always easy, company (Tinker 6). Elizabeth, on the other hand, was known in that London scene for her wit, diplomacy, wisdom, and "graciousness of manner" (Tinker 5). Her brother Edward referred to her as "a born hostess" (Robins 18), who oversaw the Thursday evening social gatherings at their Buckingham Street house in the 1890s and "managed" her husband's rough social edges. As Amy Tucker puts it, Elizabeth "seems to have supplied the social graces her husband lacked" (185). Socially, as well as professionally, they made a good team.

But even before the Pennells became an established part of the London aesthetic community, they created a minor reputation in England and the United States as prolific and respected cycle-travel writers. Their first two cycle-travel books, reprinted here, *A Canterbury Pilgrimage* and *An Italian Pilgrimage*[10], were well received by critics and achieved some commercial

Three popular cycles of the mid-1880s: From left to right, a Star bicycle, a sociable
(as in, side-by-side tandem) tricycle, and a Singer high-wheel bicycle.
[*Lorne Shields private collection*]

success in England and the United States. In addition, their extensive cycling
journalism, published in the pages of periodicals such as *The Century Magazine*,
*The Pall Mall Gazette*, *The Penny Illustrated Paper*, and *Outing*, established their
credentials as key early voices of and advocates for the growing cycling
community. In 1887, one anonymous critic credited the Pennells with offering
"by far the most important and charming literary treatment of the cycle," and
lauded their cycle writing for having "done more than any other writings about
it to rescue cycling from the common conception of it as rather a vulgar sport."
The Pennells, according to the reviewer, were to be commended for showing
just how "delightful" cycling could be (Rev. of Lord Bury's *Cycling Handbook* 5).
By the 1890s they had become, according to Pryor Dodge, "bicycling's most
famous couple" (90).

The Pennells were true pioneers of early cycling and their published work
on cycling is both a valuable historical resource and an entertaining body
of literature. Elizabeth's prose has a modern feel and a certain "sparkle," as
Jacqueline Block Williams puts it, that is "as appealing today as it was a hundred
years ago" (vii), and Joseph's illustrations now convey a quaint charm and

A typical velocipede or "boneshaker," probably from the late 1860s.
The pedals drove the front wheel, without any drive train. The striped pants
with jacket were typical garb for velocipedists.
[*Lorne Shields private collection*]

authenticity of another century. This edition aims to make some of that work
available once again, in historical context, to audiences familiar and new.

## "The Great Days of Cycling"

The mid-1880s were exciting times in the emerging world of cycling in
England, Europe, and North America. The bicycle, or *vélocipède* as it had
been known in the early days, was no longer a mere novelty, in the way that
the crude "boneshaker," the original bicycle, had been to many in the years
immediately following its invention in the 1860s. Technical innovations in
materials (lighter metals, ball bearings, seat springs) and improvements in
design, pioneered largely by British manufacturers, led to the creation of
efficient, faster, high-wheel machines that dominated the growing bicycle
market in the late 1870s and early 1880s. Versions of what would come to be
known as the "safety bicycle"—the precursor of the modern bicycle, with its
same-size wheels—were starting to appear but hadn't yet come to dominate
the scene as they would in the great bicycle boom of the 1890s.[11]

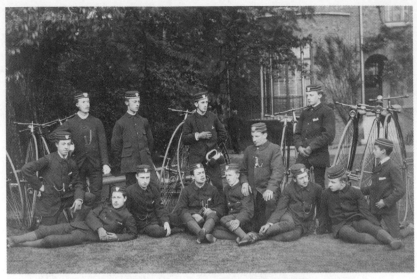

A cycling club, circa 1880. Note the military-style uniforms with caps.
The bugle held by the central figure was used to signal various riding formations.
[*Lorne Shields private collection*]

As bicycles became faster and smoother to ride in the 1870s, the number of riders grew considerably. In fact, by the late 1870s, a full-blown cycling sub-culture was beginning to emerge in England and, a few years later, in parts of the United States. At the forefront was bicycle racing, a popular spectator sport going back to the earliest days of the velocipede, but another significant factor was the rise of bicycle clubs. These were exclusive social and athletic organizations, such as the Amateur Bicycle Club and the Pickwick Bicycle Club (exclusive to London's literati), devoted to the gentlemanly pursuits of civilized exercise and socializing, as well as competition. Clubs sponsored regular weekend club rides as well as dinners, meets, and lectures. By 1878, over a dozen such clubs flourished across England (Herlihy 165). In North America, manufacturer Albert Pope and the League of American Wheelmen (LAW) led the way, and chapters of LAW sprang up in cities from Montreal to San Francisco.

Some cyclists in the late 1870s, however, were not so interested in racing or even in club rides; rather, they wanted to use their bicycles as a means to hit the road. A handful of adventurous riders, such as Charles Edward Reade (pen name "Nauticus"), Lyman Hotchkiss-Bagg (pen name "Karl Kron"),

Thomas Stevens, the celebrated high-wheel traveller, in the frontispiece from
Volume I of his *Around the World on a Bicycle*, 1887.

and, most famously, Thomas Stevens, began testing the possibilities of
long-distance cycle travel, embarking on long solo trips that they wrote about
in magazine articles and books.[12] Stevens made the biggest splash, setting off
in 1884 on a sensational near-three-year 'round-the-world adventure, which
he chronicled in the pages of *Outing* magazine and later in his popular book
*Around the World on a Bicycle* (1887). These pioneering adventure treks set the
stage for a further series of epic trans-continent and trans-world bicycle trips
in the 1890s by the likes of Frank Lenz and the adventuresome duo of Charles
Sachtleben and Thomas Allen.[13] But such grand, exotic, and often dangerous
adventures, though entertaining to read about, were not for every wheelman
or wheelwoman.

A separate sub-genre of *leisure* cycle-travel emerged in the late 1870s
involving the use of cycles to travel more modest distances, to what might be
considered more civilized destinations, staying at inns and hotels en route.
These cycle-trippers ventured on their wheels into picturesque territory or
to places of historical interest, often capturing the experience in words and
images. Accounts of this kind of early leisure cycle-travel can be found, for
instance, in the pages of *The Wheelman* magazine (later *Outing*), published in

*Cyclists' Touring Club Gazette* from July 1884, the summer the Pennells arrived in London. The tricycle advertisement reflects the prominence of tricycling at this time.
[*Lorne Shields private collection*]

Boston in 1882–1883, as well as in one of the first known leisure cycle-travel books, A.D. Chandler and J.C. Sharp's *A Bicycle Tour in England and Wales* (1881). The Bicycle Touring Club (later the Cyclists' Touring Club, or CTC), formed in 1878, was the best known of several organizations devoted to the promotion of this kind of leisure travel by bicycle. It lobbied for better roads, posted route signs, and provided resources to help members plan itineraries, find accommodation, and deal with mechanical problems on the road. "In all the principal towns of this kingdom," explained one source, "they have their 'consuls,'" who offer members "whatever help or direction they may need." Members received a uniform, badge, handbook, guide, newsletter, plus a discount and guarantee of welcome at certain inns. "No matter how covered [cyclists] may be with the mud and dust of the roads, their tickets of membership at once distinguish them from common tramps" ("From Coventry to Chester on Wheels" 646).[14]

This trade card from the mid-1880s shows a woman riding a three-track tricycle.
The two handles control steering and braking.
[*Lorne Shields private collection*]

A significant factor in the growth of leisure cycle-touring at this time
was the emergence of the tricycle.[15] What we in the west now consider to be a
machine fit only for small children and senior citizens, was, for a time in the
early 1880s, a legitimate rival to the two-wheeler.[16] Tricycles had been around
since at least the early 1870s, but were considered clunky machines. Then in
the late 1870s, English manufacturers in the Coventry area, such as James
Starley, began making rapid advances in design that led to the creation of
faster, more efficient tricycles that greatly expanded the market possibilities.
The high-wheeler (also known as the "ordinary" or the "pennyfarthing") was
not easy to ride—getting on and off was tricky, there was no brake, the design
was not amenable to Victorian women's dress, and riders were prone to falling
off mid-flight—and it was a considerable fall off a 48- or 50-inch mount. (Mark
Twain's essay "Taming the Bicycle" describes his hilariously pathetic attempts

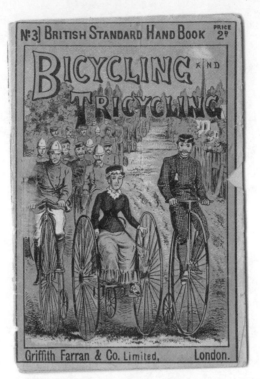

A typical early-1880s guidebook for aspiring cyclists. A guide like this would explain
how to mount, ride, and dismount the machines, as well as what to wear
while riding and how to follow cycling etiquette.
[*Lorne Shields private collection*]

to mount and ride a high-wheeler.)[17] For the most part, the ridership of the
high-wheeler was consequently confined to reasonably athletic men.

Tricycles, although not as fast as high-wheelers,[18] offered obvious
advantages to riders. Namely, they were much more stable and, therefore,
safer; they could accommodate women's clothing; and they were well suited
to socializing, in contrast to racing. As a result, cycling became much more
accessible—to women, to elderly or more conservative would-be cyclists—to
anyone, really, who could afford to buy a tricycle (which did cost considerably
more than a high-wheeler). Doctors and tradesmen began to use tricycles for
work purposes (Dodge 72). Singer produced a "carrier" model that could be
used for hauling goods. Artists and photographers found the tricycle handy for
carting around easels, stools, sketching supplies, and photography equipment
(Herlihy 212).[19]

This was the other great advantage of the tricycle: it was well suited to touring. Although some cyclists didn't let the pitfalls of the high-wheeler stop them from touring extensively (Thomas Stevens and Karl Kron being the best known[20]), it wasn't all that easy. The tricycle, though, was ideal for travelling long distances. Although its extra weight made it a challenge to propel uphill, the tricycle, in general, had closed the speed gap and was only a few miles per hour slower than the high-mount on the flat (Herlihy 214). It was much easier to stop and start (for those who wanted to take a break and admire the scenery), and it could accommodate some luggage (the Pennells carried two small bags on their luggage rack in Italy), as well as a second rider, in the case of tandem models like the ones the Pennells used, for those who preferred to travel with company. These features enabled the beginning of mainstream cycle-tourism; people of a certain social class began to embark on tricycle tours.[21] In his 1887 account of the contemporary cycling scene, Karl Kron lists several instances of married couples, including the Pennells, who travelled extensively by tricycle in the 1880s, though few besides the Pennells had written about their trips (530).[22]

When the Pennells arrived in London in the summer of 1884, they stepped into the middle of a flourishing cycling scene for which their talents as writers and illustrator were perfectly suited. Elizabeth's diary entries from this period make frequent reference to seeing bicycles and tricycles everywhere they went. Her entry for 4 August 1884, a bank holiday, for instance, describes one of her first "tricycle runs" in England with Joseph. They saw "any number of cyclers but more three than two wheelers—All sorts of machines were out and all sorts of riders riding them. Saw one or two women." Almost immediately they found work writing about, and illustrating for, cycling trips and taking part in various cycling societies and events. In her 1929 biography of her husband, Elizabeth looked back fondly on the mid-1880s: "Those were the great days of cycling. Karl Kron compiling his big book, Stevens making the world tour on his nickel-plated machine, [Dan] Canary doing his trick riding on the music-hall stage and at cycling entertainments" (LL1: 160).[23] If not for modesty, Elizabeth could easily have included herself and her husband in this list.[24]

While the tricycle broadened participation in wheeling, cycling truly started to become a broad *cultural* phenomenon in England and America only with the rise of a cycling literature in the early 1880s. At this time, we begin to see the emergence of club newsletters (such as the *CTC Gazette* in England and the *League of American Wheelmen Bulletin and Gazette*), cycling journals and

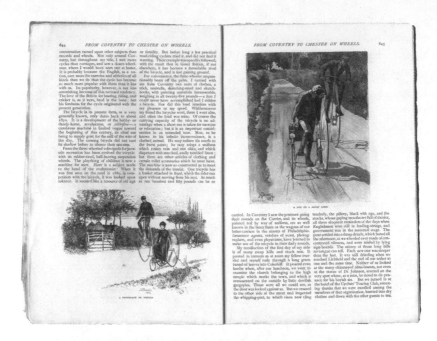

The *Century Illustrated Monthly Magazine* was a favourite venue for the Pennells'
cycle-travel writing in the 1880s. This excerpt is from the Pennells' first jointly
produced cycle-travel article, "From Coventry to Chester on Wheels," written
shortly after the Pennells arrived in England. Joseph made the trip alone on a
high-wheeler, but Elizabeth wrote the text to accompany Joseph's illustrations.
[*Lorne Shields private collection*]

magazines (such as *Bicycling*, *Bicycling World*, and Albert Pope's *The Wheelman
Illustrated* (later merged with *Outing*)),[25] individual cycling articles and poems
in newspapers, and, gradually, cycling books of various kinds—travel accounts,
how-to guides, even novels and collections of poetry.[26] Thomas Stevens
and Karl Kron were two of the most recognized voices in this early cycling
literature, but the Pennells, through both the quantity and quality of their
cycle writing, played an even more prominent role in the creation of this early
cycling culture. They were the first writer-cyclists to convincingly convey—in
both words and images—the vibrant, emerging cycling scene and the exciting
possibilities of leisure cycle travel.

## "Wife...or *Something*"

ELIZABETH ROBINS PENNELL

Elizabeth Robins was born in 1855 in Philadelphia to an established colonial family whose roots reached back several generations in Virginia and Maryland, but who were relatively new to Philadelphia. The Robins family had history and breeding but little money after the "upheaval" (Elizabeth's word) following the Civil War (*Our Philadelphia* 132).[27] When Elizabeth was a little girl, her mother died and her father, Edward Robins, who shocked his Episcopal relations by suddenly converting to Catholicism, sent Elizabeth and her sister off to live at convents, first at Conflans, in France, for one year, when Elizabeth was six, and then at Eden Hall, part of the Convent of the Sacred Heart in Torresdale, outside Philadelphia, where she spent ten more years, quite literally cloistered, surrounded by French nuns, knowing little of the city and its ways. In fact, she recalls how "there was less of Philadelphia than of France in the discipline, the devotions, and the relaxations of the convent" (92). These years at Sacred Heart, however, were remembered fondly by Elizabeth. She was, by her own account, a shy, bookish child, who was "small, plain, unbecomingly dressed and conscious of it" (36). Although Elizabeth would visit her grandfather's house in the city on occasion, the convent was, in her eyes, her "home" (188). She seems to have received an excellent, if rather European, formal education there, exposed to French manners and cuisine, French language, and the best of English and French literature.

This fine bookish education, however, gave Elizabeth little in the way of practical social education. In her typically sly fashion, she explains, "The Convent had been concerned in preparing me for society in the next world, not in this one" (*OP* 133). When she returned to Philadelphia society at age seventeen, a Catholic in a city of Protestants, in a family that had only the pretense of money, she felt the outsider, never quite fitting in with the other girls, a feeling she says she never quite grew out of (140).

Those first years back in the city after so long in the convent were a difficult transition, as Elizabeth tried to find her place in society. A key, formative event of this period of early adulthood was attending the Centennial Exposition of 1876 in Philadelphia. She refers to this as her "First Awakening" to the world of art and the possibility of travel (*OP* 205). There she, like many Americans, encountered for the first time masterpieces of world art. The streetcar to the Exposition grounds carried her "out of my world of red brick

Elizabeth Robins Pennell, circa 1890.
[*Portrait by Frederick Hollyer. Courtesy of the Victoria and Albert Museum*]

into the heart of England, and France" (226). The exhibits left her "blank and bewildered" (231), but eager to learn more and see more of the world. The Expo, she explains, "opened for me vistas hitherto undreamed of" (209). Perhaps inspired by the Exposition, she briefly tried her hand at illustration, and then working at her Uncle Charles Godfrey Leland's experimental Philadelphia Arts and Crafts school, but she quickly realized she didn't have the talent required to make a career in illustration (257).

The idea of becoming a writer was suggested to her by Leland, an eminent Philadelphia man of letters.[28] She had enjoyed writing at the convent and even tried, unsuccessfully, to publish some of her early essays and stories. Leland encouraged her to try her hand at journalism, and she had some success writing articles for Philadelphia newspapers such as the *Evening Telegraph* and the *American* and for larger popular magazines such as *The Atlantic Monthly*.[29] Leland also pushed her to write a book, having told her "that there was not a subject upon which a book could not be written if one only went about it in the right way" (*OP* 240). Elizabeth took him up on this advice and successfully pitched the idea for a biography of Mary Wollstonecraft to the Boston publisher Roberts Brothers in 1883. Her father, a broker by trade, was, at first, proud of her writing success (Robins 17) but wasn't so keen on it as a career plan. He approved of her writing so long as it was done "in the privacy of a third-story front bedroom, or of a back parlor" (*OP* 239). Marriage was still her best option, he believed. But by 1880 she was already twenty-five, which meant the window of marriage eligibility was closing. At that point Elizabeth was a self-professed "scribbler" who carried a notebook with her wherever she went. She began to see writing as her "substitute for marriage" (239), a means to a kind of independence, which she desired "above all things" (237).

Leland introduced her to the literary scene in Philadelphia. She worked as his unofficial administrative assistant, accompanying him on literary business. He introduced her to editors such as Thomas Bailey Aldrich of *The Atlantic*, as well as other writers, such as Walt Whitman, who was living in Camden, New Jersey, across the Delaware River. Elizabeth and Leland would visit the old poet at his home and "talk of poetry and people" (*Biography of Charles Godfrey Leland* 2: 192); the "old Bohemian" (2: 193) Whitman "always wanted to hear about the gypsies" (2: 192), which were Leland's, and soon to be Elizabeth's, passion. As Elizabeth later recalled, "we were really all three very congenial and Gypsyish" (2: 193).

But Leland himself was much more of a literary influence on Elizabeth than Whitman ever was. She enjoyed the famous old poet's company, but kept silent on his poetry. Elizabeth's literary tastes tended more to the eighteenth century, while Whitman's verse, of course, anticipated the twentieth. In this, Leland and Elizabeth were kindred spirits. He was well read, with a reverence for the Augustans. And as a writer himself, Leland was remarkably prolific, first as a journalist, and later as a writer of books on a wide variety of subjects, from travel to gypsies to philosophy. His work ethic seems to have rubbed off on his niece, who would go on to write even more than Leland did and about an even broader range of subjects.

## Quaker, Artist, Cyclist
JOSEPH PENNELL

Joseph was born in Philadelphia in 1857 to a Quaker family that gave little encouragement to the young boy's artistic inclinations. But he was fiercely independent even then and ventured off to art school in the 1870s where he was introduced to the art of etching and began to study the European masters. Attending the Philadelphia Centennial Exposition of 1876 was a formative experience for the young Pennell too. Like Elizabeth, he was also entranced by the European masterworks of art. But by the late 1870s, the industrious Pennell had given up art school, after bristling under the authority of what he saw as wrong-headed masters, and taken to scraping up paid illustration work, often "running to fires" in the city, so he could dash off a quick sketch that he might sell to a newspaper (*LL1*: 41).

Around this same time, Pennell also discovered the other great passion of his life. In his autobiography, *Adventures of an Illustrator* (1925), he recalls how in 1875, at the age of eighteen, he first tried riding a boneshaker bicycle owned by one of the neighbour boys (29). A few years later, in 1878, he bought his first bicycle, likely a high-wheel, and spent his days riding the bike and his nights attending art school (53). By the early 1880s, he was exploring the social cycling scene in Philadelphia, which Elizabeth remembers as "a period of great cycling meets, big cycling dinners, and amazing cycling parades" (*LL1*: 36–37). Joseph became an early member of the League of American Wheelmen and Captain and Secretary of the Germantown Bicycle Club (*Adventures* 58). An avid rider and energetic administrator, Joseph established a solid reputation in Philadelphia cycling circles. He recalled later, "This was at the beginning of bicycling, and in it I was a much greater person than in art" (59).

But not for long. By the early 1880s, Pennell had begun to be known as a hard-working, talented illustrator. He secured commissions to illustrate books as well as magazine pieces, and took on some travelling work for *The Century* and other publishers. He began to be invited to take part in etching exhibitions and joined the Society of Philadelphia Etchers. Although New York and Boston were the undeniable centres of American magazine publishing at this time, Philadelphia was home to some major players such as *Lippincott's* and *The Ladies' Home Journal*. Soon enough, Pennell was gaining attention and getting all the work he could handle.

Joseph Pennell in the Buckingham Street Dining Room, circa 1895.
[*Photograph by Elliot and Fry*]

Pennell had the good fortune to enter the working world of illustration
at the perfect moment. The American magazine industry was experiencing a
period of extraordinary growth. In 1865, about 700 magazines operated in the
United States. By 1880, that number had more than tripled to reach 2,400, and
by 1885, over 3,300 (Tebbel and Zuckerman 57). The most popular of these had
huge circulation numbers: 100,000 for *Harper's* and 200,000 for *The Century*
(formerly *Scribner's*) by 1885 (60). Illustration was a big part of the success
of these magazines. Unlike England, where illustrated magazines such as
*Cornhill* and *Once a Week* had thrived since the 1840s, in the United States,
widespread magazine illustration really only took off in the 1870s, with
improvements in the technical production process and the emergence of
a magazine-reading culture. Quickly, readers came to expect high-quality
illustrations. Big magazines like *The Century* and *Harper's* employed their

own staff of illustrators. That meant that by the early 1880s, when Pennell came along, there was tremendous demand for talented illustrators.

## "The Romance of Work"[30]

Joseph Pennell and Elizabeth Robins met in the summer of 1881 in Philadelphia when Joseph was commissioned by *Scribner's* to do a series of illustrations for a piece to be called "Rambles in Old Philadelphia." *Scribner's* editor Richard Gilder asked Charles Godfrey Leland to write the accompanying story, but Leland, who was busy with other projects, proposed that his twenty-six-year-old niece, who was trying to make a go of being a writer, pen the article in his stead. Gilder agreed and sent Elizabeth with Leland to meet the artist she would be working with. Elizabeth later recalled her initial impressions of Pennell in his studio where they met: he exuded a "strange combination of shyness and self-possession" and was somewhat awkward in conversation at first, but "as he talked he fired one with the flame of his enthusiasm" for art (*LL*1: 47).

With their project in mind, Joseph offered to take Elizabeth on walks to see the old buildings, many of them lesser-known gems, he had sketched for the piece and loved so much. They shared a love of walking and of art, and exploring the city's architecture together on foot every day laid the foundation for friendship, collaborative work, and eventually romance. As Elizabeth recalls, these walks were a "revelation" (*LL*1: 48); she felt like she was seeing the city for the first time (*OP* 282).

Thus began a somewhat unconventional courtship. As Elizabeth put it, "We quickly understood each other" (*LL*1: 48). Following the *Scribner's* piece, they worked together again on an illustrated article for a new Philadelphia magazine, *Our Continent*, and began scheming a joint book project about Philadelphia's historic buildings as well as other projects, both independent and joint. Soon, however, work would separate them.

Pennell accepted a job that would see him spend the winter of 1881–1882 in New Orleans, creating illustrations for George W. Cable's *Century* series on Creole culture. In person Joseph may have been shy and awkward, but in his letters during this period he is playful, brash, and fiercely encouraging of Elizabeth's independent career as a writer. "Don't allow yourself to be drawn away from Literature on any account" (*LL*1: 57), he implores her in a letter from 19 February 1882. Elsewhere in these letters he dreams of numerous collaborative projects.

Another important part of their courtship involves their shared fascination with gypsy culture. In those days, West Philadelphia happened to be on the migratory route of Romany caravans that travelled between Florida and Maine. In the spring and summer of 1882, Joseph and Elizabeth "caught the Romany fever" (*LL1*: 70) after being introduced to "gypsyism" by her Uncle Leland, who had written extensively about them. For Leland, "gypsying" was part sport, part hobby, and all passion. Visiting gypsy camps with Leland and attempting to learn the Romany language together became a favourite pastime in the early relationship of Joseph and Elizabeth. She had "come under the spell" of the "charm of the Gypsy" (*Biography of Charles Godfrey Leland* 1: 124).

This interest in gypsies was no passing fad for the Pennells. When Joseph visited Italy in 1883, he wrote a letter to Elizabeth explaining how excited he was to encounter real "Roms"; he eagerly tried out his scraps of Romany language, much to their bemusement and confusion (*LL1*: 87). In all three of their tricycle books, Elizabeth and Joseph document encounters with gypsies and remark on their sense of kinship with them. Their personal correspondence in the 1880s is sprinkled with Romany phrases. In 1891, the Pennells wrote a book, *To Gipsyland*, about their bicycle pilgrimage from Paris to Hungary, the true homeland of the Romany. In a way, this was the most significant of many pilgrimages for the Pennells. "No more beautiful month of our life together can I recall," Elizabeth writes in her biography of her husband (235). Their gypsy fascination was a vogue of the age, certainly (ever since George Borrow's *The Romany Rye* (1857)), but there was something deeper in the Pennells' personalities that made them identify with gypsies. The Pennells were roamers; they spent most of their adult lives away from Philadelphia. They were based for a long period in London, but they travelled extensively and often throughout Europe, on the road for months at a time before circling back to London. She once told a puzzled gypsy in France (speaking in Romany, no less) that she herself was "a Gipsy come from over the seas" (*Our Sentimental Journey* 40).

They got married in Philadelphia in 1884, but even that event was uncon-ventional. Elizabeth speaks of it as a kind of practical arrangement, proposed by Joseph, as a way of making their travelling together less complicated. With a trip to Italy in the works, an unmarried man and woman travelling together were sure to encounter problems. Joseph "suggested a life partnership which would enable us henceforward to share not simply Italy's but the world's beauty, at no risk of criticism or gossip" (*LL1*: 107). The secular ceremony took place in her family's home, since both of them were estranged from their religious roots, his Quakerism and her Catholicism.

From *To Gipsyland* (1893), the Pennells' account of a cycle trip from Paris to Hungary in 1891. By this time, they had traded their tandem tricycle for a pair of safety bicycles.

## Tandem Efforts

COLLABORATION

When it comes to their professional life, their relationship was highly unusual for the time. It was a kind of work-and-play partnership that was a remarkably equal arrangement based on their shared belief that intellectual work mattered most. As Elizabeth explains, they agreed on a mutual and mostly equal prime directive: "not to allow anything to interfere with his drawing and my writing. Should they call us in different directions, each must go his or her own way" (*LL1*: 123). And they did just that, many times working apart from each other for months at a go. "He went his way, I went mine," she says (*LL1*: 275). Although Joseph enjoyed the greater reputation, he never downplayed Elizabeth's talents. In fact, he realized that Elizabeth was the better writer, and he wasn't shy about asking for her writerly assistance (*LL1*: 50). She didn't always get the bylines she deserved but that seems to have been largely by her own choice.

The exact nature of their collaborative creative process isn't always easy to determine. With their joint projects, the most common arrangement seems to have involved Elizabeth writing and Joseph illustrating, but as Meaghan Clarke puts it, their "entangled identities and contributions are difficult to unravel" (123). With their early cycle-travel books, his name generally appears first on the title page and spine, even though the books are written in Elizabeth's first-person voice, and despite the fact that illustrators were generally given subordinate status to the author of an illustrated work.[31] This may have been a strategic choice on their part. Joseph was better known and he was a male author; given the context—writing about cycling—it may have been seen as an advantage to play up Joseph's authorial role, and downplay Elizabeth's.

When it comes to works attributed solely to Joseph, the matter is complicated by the fact that Elizabeth took dictation for him, and that she seems to have had an extensive role in writing out and editing his work. Not only that, she appears to have written some of the work actually attributed to him. We know of one instance early in their time together when she wrote a magazine article in her husband's voice.[32] Another time, she writes to tell him of another cycling article she'd submitted to a magazine: "I have signed your name because I think if you are willing to own the paper, it comes better from you than from me" (Pennell-Whistler Collection, box 307).[33] Joseph seems to have gone along with this, but he encouraged her to use her own name: "I send back the mss—with lots of corrections and much surprise as usual at your knowledge—sign your name—I don't want the credit for what I haven't done" (qtd. in Clarke 125). Yet Elizabeth's diaries and letters from the 1880s and 1890s make numerous references to her writing "notes" for "cycling papers," in particular for weekly columns in *The Pall Mall Gazette* and *The Penny Illustrated Paper*—short pieces that appeared under a pseudonym or without a byline at all but which many readers would have assumed were penned by Joseph. In an 1889 letter to her husband she jokes about this:

All my cycling notes are off—proofs came from PMG [*Pall Mall Gazette*] last night—and now I can draw a breath of relief. Everyone will say how serious C.Y.C. and A. Wheeler [pseudonyms used in the cycling column] has suddenly grown...this morning came a note from [Clement] Shorter with a card for an exhibition he wants you to puff, he says your contributions to the Penny Illustrated [sic] are charming. (P-WC, box 305)

Elizabeth's underlining of "your" implies they have a little secret: she is the one who is doing the writing.[34]

Their collaboration extended to publishing matters as well. Elizabeth's diaries reveal that she took the lead in some of the negotiations with publishers, usually when Joseph was off working abroad. She was also heavily involved in handling the publisher's proofs of their articles and books. She even attended some meetings of cycling societies, and, on occasion, addressed them. Only very occasionally in her diaries is there a suggestion that she resents her husband getting most of the recognition while she does much of the work. In an entry dated 8 February 1888 she comments on a review in *The Pall Mall Gazette* of their third cycling book, *Our Sentimental Journey*, noting "all the praise given to Joseph," with "myself being given a back seat as it were." Her choice of metaphor is ironically apt, since on their tandem tricycle, as in much of their collaborative process, Elizabeth was, in fact, very much in the lead. In recognition of her lead role, and in keeping with the modern practice of putting the writer's name before the illustrator's, this edition reverses the order of the Pennells' names on the title page.

## A Canterbury Pilgrimage

In June of 1884, the Pennells were off to London, Joseph having been commissioned by *The Century* to do a series of cathedral illustrations in England and France. London would serve as their base and enable them to make local contacts that they hoped would lead to more work for both of them. But the Pennells had plans for play as well as work: a cycling trip together in Italy, an endeavour Joseph had been scheming since an earlier visit to Italy with William Dean Howells in 1883.[35] The Pennells purchased a Coventry Rotary Convertible[36] tandem tricycle, a machine they had tried out in Philadelphia before they left America, and made preparations to depart for Italy in late summer.[37]

When a cholera scare caused postponement of the Italy trip, the Pennells struck on the idea of a short cycling jaunt from London to Canterbury, where Joseph had been commissioned to do some drawings for *The Portfolio*. Elizabeth saw this as an opportunity for her to "gain practice" on the new tricycle before the longer Italian journey they still hoped to do. In addition, the Pennells figured that if they followed the route of Chaucer's pilgrims, they might be able to sell the illustrated story of the trip to a magazine. Literary pilgrimages were a popular form of travel literature in the nineteenth century. As Nicola J. Watson explains, it was the "period which first saw the practice of visiting places

Cover of the Pennells' first cycle-travel book.
It appeared in train station bookstalls across England.

associated with Anglophone authors in order to savour book, place, and their interrelations" (2). Readers enjoyed accounts of literary pilgrims' visits to famous authors' graves, birthplaces, carefully preserved homes, and "whole imaginary literary territories, such as 'Dickens' London' or 'Hardy's Wessex'" (3).[38]

The short trip was a delight for the Pennells, leisurely exploring for the first time the countryside of Kent, "two [it was actually three] days of loafing along its windy roads, up and down its gentle hills, through its sleepy villages, between its cherry and hop gardens" (*LL1*: 123). While Elizabeth wrote up the narrative of the journey, Joseph studied old manuscripts in the British Museum, searching for inspiration for some of the medieval-inspired illustrations he would eventually include in the book (137).

Joseph pitched the piece to *The Century*, but its editors were hesitant to take it on, fearing an overload of Pennell material in their pages. The *English Illustrated* turned them down too. But Richmond Seeley, of *Portfolio*, was intrigued by Joseph's unusual illustrations and, after reading Elizabeth's manuscript, agreed to publish it as a short book which he would put out "in a paper cover for a shilling" and sell "on all the railway bookstalls" around England (*LL1*: 137).

The book was published in London in the late summer of 1885, with a dedication to Robert Louis Stevenson, whose breezy, literate, self-deprecating travel writing was clearly an inspiration for theirs. Shortly after, Scribner's in the United States issued an American edition.[39] The book was, as Elizabeth later put it, "an immediate success" (*LL1*: 149). According to Karl Kron, it was "praised by the wheel press of both countries" (687). Andrew Lang, in the popular *Daily News*, gave it a ringing headline: "The Most Wonderful Shillingsworth Modern Literature has to Offer" (qtd. in *LL1*: 149). A reviewer in *The Graphic* called it "one of the prettiest illustrated books, which has been published for some time." The Pennells' "adventures were few," the reviewer continued, "but in the true spirit of romance they detect interest and character in the commonest affairs" (247).

Reviewers in the United States also praised the book for its "quaint designs" and "simple and charming manner, with a pleasant flavor of fun." One Boston paper recommended it as "an odd and highly entertaining little book" ("Literary Review" 6). A San Francisco paper praised the way the authors "make interesting the experiences of three uneventful days" ("Current Literature"). It was "well worth its price, fifty cents, for the drawings" alone. Boston's *Outing* magazine called the book "delightful" and warned that upon reading it "the longing grows upon one to beg, buy or appropriate a tandem, and with wife or 'sister' make the experience all his own" ("A Canterbury Pilgrimage").[40] Finally, Robert Underwood Johnson, an associate editor at *The Century*, reported to the Pennells in London that "the *Pilgrimage* was a great success at home." Elizabeth writes in her diary that, according to Johnson, "It [the book] had given us a place in American literature" (Diary, vol. 3, 9 Dec. 1885).

Congratulatory letters poured in from friends and strangers. The Pickwick Bicycle Club invited Joseph to give a talk about the book, as did the Shakespeare Society. And best of all, as far as the Pennells were concerned, they received a short appreciative note from the book's dedicatee, Robert Louis Stevenson, in which he writes that he admires their "graceful" volume (Booth and Mehew 121). Looking back at those days, Elizabeth recalls, "We made a hit, no mistake, and it was great fun" (*LL1*: 150).

The book sold well—over 12,000 copies in the first year in England alone.[41] For a while it was the talk of the cycling community. In September 1885, Joseph took part in a cycle race in Harrogate and wrote to Elizabeth to tell her that "Everybody had seen 'The Pilgrimage,' and most had read it" (qtd. in *LL1*: 152). At cycling society meetings, Joseph, and occasionally even a mortified Elizabeth, were asked to speak about their adventure.[42] Without intending to, the Pennells found themselves considered experts, almost accidental authorities on all matters of the wheel.

## "Voila, a Reputation"

The commercial and critical success of *A Canterbury Pilgrimage* established the Pennells' reputation in the cycling world certainly, and, to some extent, even beyond—into the literary one. For several years after the book's initial publication, Joseph and Elizabeth inherited the unofficial nicknames "the Canterbury Pilgrims." Elizabeth's diaries from this period tell numerous stories of encounters with strangers who were fans of their book or at least had heard of them because of it. Her diary entry of 28 August 1886, for instance, describes an encounter in Yorkshire with a visiting Harvard professor and his wife. "Mrs. Moore said someone had told her a lady and gentleman had just come to Lincoln on their tricycle on which they had been travelling all over England and she at once said it must be Mr. and Mrs. Pennell—Voila [sic], a reputation." The book had such a high profile, available on bookstalls everywhere, that it seemed almost everyone had at least heard of "the Americans who wrote the Canterbury Pilgrimage," as more than one acquaintance described them (Diary, Mrs. Church, 22 May 1887). In another diary entry from 3 July 1889, Elizabeth recounts how when George Allen, a well-known London publisher, was introduced to her he inquired if she was the "Mrs. Pennell of cycling fame."

Part of this reputation entailed receiving visiting cycle-tourists, especially other Americans, who stopped in London while on their own cycling travels. The Pennells were seen by many fellow touring cyclists, especially husband and wife teams, as cycle-travel pioneers, and thus their London residence became a kind of pilgrimage site of its own. Elizabeth's diary records several meetings with such pilgrims. ("Mr. and Mrs. Harold Lewis of Philadelphia called in the afternoon—Just back from a tricycle ride of 2200 miles, beating our record all to pieces" (Elizabeth's London Diary, 24 Sep. 1887).) Some thanked the Pennells for inspiring their own cycling travels. For instance, after one of Joseph's lectures at Bedford Park, "Two or three people...had much to say about cycling and how our books sent them off on cycling tours" (London Diary, 15 Feb. 1890).

Why was the Pennells' first book such a hit? Timing accounts for much. The book appeared at the height of the tricycle's glory days in England in the mid-1880s, before the emerging safety bicycle offered another viable option for those seeking accessible social and touring cycling. Readers were curious about cycling in general and its potential for leisure travel in particular. Published accounts of cycle-tours, especially book-length ones, were still something of a novelty.[43] Cycle travel tapped into an interest in, perhaps even a nostalgia for, alternate forms of travel in an age so dominated by the railroad. (The success of Stevenson's *Travels with a Donkey in the Cévennes*, for instance, was partly due to the way it deliberately reached back to an older mode of transport.) People in the mid-1880s were intrigued by cycling as a new form of travel that combined the pace of old-fashioned horse-and-carriage travel with an element of modernity.

The Pennells were also smart to aim for a broad audience—two audiences, really, as Elizabeth later pointed out: "the cycling public at a period when cycling was then popular sport; [and] to the scholarly public as a tribute to Chaucer and his Pilgrims" (*LL1*: 149). The avid "cycling public" was certainly keen to get its hands on any cycling literature. But the Pennells were careful to point out in their preface that they were only semi-serious cyclists, cycle-tourists rather than cycle-*racers*, "pilgrims not scorchers."[44] Therefore, they made an effort to appeal to more than cycling fanatics. The Pennells explain that they chose not to bore their readers with specific details of routes or other technical aspects of their endeavour that were found in some cycling literature. The preface specifically addresses the "non-cyclers" who might pick up the book, those who might just appreciate a good story—which happens to involve tricycles.

Before the Pennells, cycling travel narratives had been rare, and those that did exist, like A.D. Chandler's *A Bicycle Tour in England and Wales* and the "Nauticus" books, tended to be largely descriptive and not particularly literary. The Pennells, however, struck on a unique and winning formula for the time: taking the literate, slightly satirical, picturesque style of travel writing[45] popularized by Robert Louis Stevenson in *Travels with a Donkey in the Cévennes* and giving it a tricycle twist.[46] Readers of *A Canterbury Pilgrimage*, like fans of Stevenson's book, enjoyed the light but literary tone. Sprinkled throughout the account are literary allusions, not only to Chaucer but also to Shakespeare, Swift, Dickens, and Greek mythology. The Kentish landscape provided plenty of instances of the picturesque, and the Pennells had a talent for conveying through words and images both the rough architecture and rustic but seemingly authentic life of tramps, hop-pickers, and labourers in a manner reminiscent of Wordsworth's sympathetic portrayal of earlier rustics. And like Stevenson, the Pennells didn't take themselves too seriously as travellers, occasionally poking fun at their own ineptness with their tricycle and mocking over-serious "cyclers" they encountered en route. Yet Elizabeth captures, perhaps better than any writer before her, the joy of the cycling experience:

"We rode on with light hearts. An eternity of wheeling through such perfect country and in such soft sunshine would, we thought, be the true earthly paradise" (46).

The book also appealed to a scholarly, literary crowd as much as to a cycling one. In this age of "readerly tourism," a sizable literary reading public appreciated Elizabeth's many allusions to Chaucer's classic. Her convent education had left her with a solid grasp of the classics, and she clearly knew her Chaucer, sprinkling quotations and references to *The Canterbury Tales* throughout their pilgrimage account. One Dr. Frederick J. Furnivall, a Chaucer scholar (and founder of the Chaucer Society in 1868) and an avid cyclist himself, was so impressed by the Pennells' book that he sought out an invitation, and soon became fast friends with the American couple and a regular visitor at their flat.[47] Chaucer wasn't the only literary attraction of the book. Elizabeth also appeals to more contemporary tastes with numerous references to the works and life of Charles Dickens, who spent some formative years in the Rochester area and used it as a setting for several of his novels.

The fact that the Pennells were Americans writing about England probably didn't hurt either. Like many American travellers before them, the Pennells brought a fresh perspective to a much-described English landscape. As Keppel puts it, "Things that were ordinary matters of course to the native Londoners... were to the young American couple intensely interesting novelties" (21).

And, finally, the book's design and Joseph's illustrations deserve considerable credit for the book's success. Paper covers were a relatively new feature in English books and the proportions and design of the book were unconventional. As a result, Elizabeth explains, it stood out on railway book-stalls and bookshop windows (*LL1*: 149). Joseph's illustrations were not only of a high quality, they were also unusual—a combination of conventional contemporary illustrations of landscapes together with highly stylized Chauceresque medieval images, sometimes both at the same time, like the image from the first page that features medieval pilgrims on horseback facing off against their Victorian counterparts on steel steeds. Given these design features and the modest price, it's easy to see why the book sold so well.

## An Italian Pilgrimage/Two Pilgrims' Progress

The idea for the Pennells' first joint trip to Italy came from Joseph's visit there in 1883 on assignment to create illustrations for W.D. Howells's *Tuscan Cities*. Up to that point, Joseph had travelled only within the United States, and the most exotic (and most European) destination he had visited had been New Orleans in 1882. Italy was a revelation. His letters to Elizabeth from this period capture his astonishment at the beauty of Italian landscape and architecture. As Elizabeth explains, Joseph was "an American youth for the first time under the spell of an Italy which was not yet a hapless prey to tourists and progress— the youth with eyes wide open to beauty, with no ambition but to capture that beauty and imprison it on paper or copper plate" (*LL1*: 82).

With Howells he visited Florence and several small Tuscan towns such as Siena and Urbino. In letters to Elizabeth, Joseph writes, "I believe that if I should stay here I wouldn't do anything—but look at this lovely land—for it is too beautiful to touch" (*LL1*: 89). But Joseph was incapable of only staring for long; he immersed himself in work. Later they took in Venice. Joseph reported back to a friend, "I feel simply crushed by the amount of material around me" (100); to Elizabeth he laments how "the country is overpowering—everything is worth drawing" (85). He implores her: "[Y]ou must get over here—we could do such loads of things" (84). They could both get more than enough work to pay for a long stay, he claimed. Magazines back in London and the United States would surely snap up their illustrated stories on Italian towns and culture. Howells's book was just the start. When they came up with the idea for a tandem tricycle trip from Florence to Rome is hard to say. In a letter from 1884, Joseph mentions their planning of the Italy trip, lining up work to do there, and he refers to "Ye Pilgrimage to Rome" (113).

With the cholera scare over, the Pennells set off via train from London on 12 October 1884 with a new machine, having exchanged their Coventry Rotary for a tandem Humber, "a better designed, better looking machine, [which] did not fail us from beginning to end" (*LL1*: 129).[48] The journey was an auspicious occasion, one they had dreamt of, talked of, and planned for over a year—not to mention "the immediate reason for our marriage" (128). Joseph was eager to finally share the "loveliness" of Italy with Elizabeth, to show her all his favourite spots (128). Friends had warned them about the notorious difficulties of Italian travel (the bad food, dishonest landlords, comfortless hotels) but "these prophecies only added to the sense of adventure" (129). In the end, it was a "perfect" trip. The roads were surprisingly good; the October weather was excellent. Not even their arrest in Rome at the end of their trip (for "some infringement of cycling regulation") could overshadow what Elizabeth calls "the most beautiful, the most successful of the many beautiful, successful journeys we were to take together" (130).

In Italy, the Pennells didn't follow a particular literary route the way they did in England. Rather, they invoked a general sense of spiritual pilgrimage to the "celestial city" of Rome, though there's little of the spiritual in their account. (In this sense, they employ a partly ironic, secular use of the term "pilgrimage," reminiscent of Mark Twain's *An Innocent Abroad: Or, The New Pilgrim's Progress* (1869).) Though they make passing reference to literary figures whose stomping grounds they pass through en route (such as Boccaccio and Virgil), no single literary guide leads them. The prefatory poem by Leland plays up the spiritual pilgrimage motif with several references to John Bunyan's *Pilgrim's Progress*, suggesting that the Pennells' book is, in fact, a kind of respectful parody of the famous Christian allegory. But in the English edition especially, the Pennells drop this literary thread save for occasional mentions of Bunyan's protagonist. The American edition, published as *Two Pilgrims' Progress*, makes more effort to emphasize the Bunyanesque element of the pilgrimage, not only with the title but also with the addition of chapter epigraphs from *The Pilgrim's Progress*, but this nod to the great classic of pilgrimage literature feels largely gratuitous. For the most part, only a tenuous connection exists between the Bunyan epigraphs and the content of the travel narrative.[49]

The response to the "Italian book" was something of a let-down after the wild success of their first book. Reviews were mostly positive, praising Elizabeth's "delightful" and "chatty" prose and the "light and pleasant touch" of Joseph's illustrations (Rev. of *An Italian Pilgrimage* 3).[50] One newspaper, *The York Herald*, even claimed that the book's "sales and criticism show it is proving even more popular than *A Canterbury Pilgrimage*" (5), but some other reviewers found the book "disappointing" ("Light Travel" 701).[51] Elizabeth's diaries do include one anecdote that is reminiscent of the response to *A Canterbury Pilgrimage*— 24 March 1888: "I met a Miss Cummins who told me of a friend of hers who made a walking tour over our route in Italy shortly after our ride—Wherever he went, he heard of us and our tricycle which seemed to have made a tremendous impression on people." But while the Pennells may have made an impression, the book, in terms of sales, did not. Regarding the English edition, Seeley described the sales as "disappointing"; T. Niles of Roberts Brothers, the American edition publisher, went even further, calling them "disastrous" (Diary, 7 Feb. 1887).

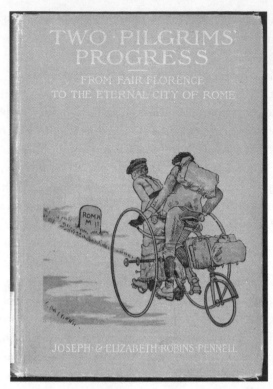

Cover of *Two Pilgrims' Progress*, the American edition of the Pennells' Italy book.

The success of *A Canterbury Pilgrimage* was a hard act to follow, but the mixed response to the Italian book is difficult to explain. The Pennells' ambivalence toward religion and their shift in mood toward the end of the book, when they seem grumpy and occasionally exasperated by mechanical troubles with their tricycle and the generally unfriendly reactions of some of the Umbrians they encountered close to Rome, might account for part of this. Successful pilgrimages are supposed to end with a sense of renewal, but the Pennells' journey ends on an ironic note, somewhat sourly, with the Pennells being fined by the local *carabinieri* for riding their tricycle on the streets of Rome. There's little sense of the pilgrims exalting in the kind of spiritual benefit usually associated with the end of a pilgrimage.[52]

Yet the Italian book has considerable literary merit—more, in some ways, than the more successful *A Canterbury Pilgrimage*. It exudes a substance, depth, a sureness of tone, an engagement with the landscape, culture, and history of a place that is only hinted at in the more superficial *Canterbury Pilgrimage*. Elizabeth relates several memorable episodes, from the account of their dreamy "golden" days spent at the monastery in Monte Oliveto, to the hilariously bad marionette show in Siena, to the encounter with a dandified Italian cyclist, Sandrino, who suffers from "the English fever." One big difference in Italy was the novelty of the Pennells' tricycle. Again and again the locals express astonishment at the Pennells' machine, having never seen a tricycle before, let alone a tandem one. Crowds gather to gawk in every village; children want to touch it; at one point, an encroaching mob threatens to get ugly, until a local man with a stick intervenes to save the day. Perhaps the most compelling feature of *An Italian Pilgrimage* is the way it captures so vividly the pains and pleasures of cycle-touring. All cyclists can relate to Elizabeth's accounts of the grind of steep uphills (some of which required them to dismount and push the heavy tricycle) as well as the transcendent joy of a stiff tailwind propelling a machine effortlessly at great speed. Today's machines may be lighter and stronger, but the fundamental experience of cycling hasn't changed much since the Pennells depicted it so vividly.

The disappointing reaction to *An Italian Pilgrimage* may simply have been a result of shifting tastes. The novelty of tricycle-travel may have worn off, such that the public was already looking for other diversions. By 1886, there was a new literary cycling sensation, Thomas Stevens, whose reports on his round-the-world-on-a-high-wheel adventure were appearing in American newspapers.[53] New safety bicycle models such as the Kangaroo were beginning to catch on, and it could be that the tricycle's brief day in the sun was already coming to a close.[54]

## Further Adventures

The Pennells went on to publish one more tricycle-touring book, *Our Sentimental Journey* (1887), about another literary pilgrimage, this time through France in the footsteps of Laurence Sterne's 1767 classic. However, this last tricycle book, while also entertaining and beautifully illustrated, lacks some of the early enthusiasm of their first two cycle books, when the sense of newness, discovery, and novelty of cycle travel was still so fresh. Elizabeth admits as much in a diary entry of 8 February 1888, when she reflects on their struggles to find a publisher for the France book: "How our enthusiasm [for tricycle writing] has waned since the Canterbury Pilgrimage days." In fact, in 1887, when planning yet another literary pilgrimage, this time to Scotland in the

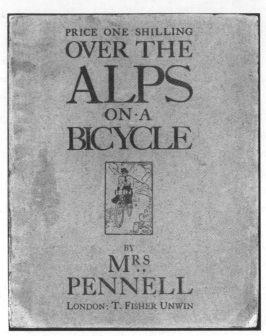

PRICE ONE SHILLING
OVER THE
ALPS
ON·A
BICYCLE

BY
MRS
PENNELL
LONDON: T. FISHER UNWIN

Cover of the Pennells' final cycle-travel book, from 1898.

footsteps of Dr. Johnson through the Hebrides, the Pennells decided to take a walking tour, "fearing that the public might weary of our tricycle" (*LL1*: 192).[55] The France book sold reasonably well, but it would be their last tricycle book. The emergence of the safety bicycle in the late 1880s, however, gave the Pennells renewed interest in cycle travel and cycle writing, and in the 1890s they embarked on a new series of cycling adventures, this time on two wheels instead of three. Their first safety-bicycle-trip book, *To Gipsyland* (1892), features a cross-Europe pilgrimage to find "real" gypsies in Hungary. Their final cycling volume, *Over the Alps on a Bicycle* (1898), presents a short, sharp account of their impressive crossing of ten mountain passes in Switzerland. During this period they also continued to churn out cycling pieces for magazines at an impressive rate, publishing articles about cycle trips through Yorkshire, Germany, and northern Italy, among other places. In all, the Pennells continued to write about their cycle-travels for close to two decades after the publication of their first two cycling books.

Despite her prominent role in the cycling community and cycling press, Elizabeth did not take an active role in the controversies connecting cycling with early feminist movements of the 1890s. In some ways she epitomized the "New Woman" stereotype that was both celebrated and satirized in the 1890s. That she chose Mary Wollstonecraft as the subject of her first book suggests at least some interest in women's rights.[56] In her own life and career, she exhibited an unconventional independence in her devotion to working after her marriage, and in her mostly equal marriage arrangement with Joseph. She more than held her own in the male-dominated realms of journalism, art criticism, publishing, and cycling. And she wrote at least one article encouraging women specifically to take up cycling as a sport.[57]

In other ways, Elizabeth was something of a conservative when it came to politics. The travel she wrote about was almost always done with her husband by her side. She skirted the Rational Dress movement altogether. She had her doubts about socialism, a favourite topic among the Pennells' social circle in London. Although she knew other professional women writers, such as Vernon Lee and Mary Robinson, she expressed little sense of solidarity with their predicament. She could be dismissive of the suffragette movement in the 1890s:

> Theoretically, I believe that women of property and position should have their vote and that men without should not, but I think it a lesser evil for women to be denied the vote than for the suffrage to become as universal for women as for men. (*Our House* 329)

In fact, she went so far as to complain about the ruckus caused by suffragette protests in her neighbourhood.[58] Any association we may wish to see between Elizabeth Robins Pennell and Victorian feminism is in her deeds more so than in her political commentary.

The Pennells appear to have stopped cycling in their early fifties. The latest published account of one of their trips dates from 1902, when Elizabeth would have been almost fifty years old.[59] In her 1897 retrospective article "Twenty Years of Cycling," Elizabeth looks back on their cycling careers and offers what amounts to a kind of manifesto of their semi-serious approach to cycle-touring. Elizabeth insists that high-risk, extreme adventure was never their goal:

> We never attempted to compete with Mr. Thomas Stevens, who first went round the world on a tall bicycle...; our ambition rather was to visit, on the wheel, places that we wished to see. We never ventured to

invade unridable [sic] continents, or even counties, if we could help it; we preferred to explore countries where our machines would carry us—not where we should have to carry them—and where there were civilized beds and food and comfort. ("Twenty Years" 188–89)

In other words, the Pennells were interested in the way cycling enabled a new type of leisure travel.

And in exploring the possibilities of cycle-tourism, they were, indeed, as Elizabeth claims, "pioneers of cycle touring in most countries of Europe." In a sense they were early ambassadors of the wheel, "preparing the way," as Elizabeth puts it, for others who would follow in their wheel tracks ("Twenty Years" 189). And others did. Contemporary married couples such as Grenville Cole and his wife, as well as Fanny and William Workman and Charles and Lillian S.M. Willis, carried on the husband-and-wife riding/writing tradition in the 1890s.[60] This cycling-couple convention remained strong throughout the twentieth century. Although writers such as Eric Newby or Jill Savage may not have been aware of the Pennells' work when they penned their husband-wife cycle-travel books generations later, a direct, if unacknowledged, line connects the Pennells' books to such modern cycling classics as *Round Ireland in Low Gear* (1987) and *Miles from Nowhere* (1983). Similarly, the light humour and literary pilgrimage motif of the Pennells' books show up again in Charles S. Brooks's *A Thread of English Road* (1924) and Bernard Newman's cycling books of the 1930s and 1940s, such as *In the Trail of the Three Musketeers* (1934).

Were they around today, "those Pennells" would be pleased to learn that their own accounts of cycling pilgrimages still inspire later generations of cycling pilgrims to trace their very routes, in much the same way they followed writers before them. In September 1984, for instance, on the centenary of the Pennells' Canterbury trip, a group of cyclists from the Southern Veteran-Cycle Club in England re-created the original ride (as close as possible) on period tricycles and boneshakers.[61] More recently in Tuscany, a bicycle touring company offered an eleven-day guided bicycle trip along what they call "the Pennell Trail," tracing much of the couple's original route from Florence to Rome.[62]

The Pennells would no doubt also be delighted to learn how popular leisure cycle-travel has become around the world. Cycle-touring is, perhaps, more prevalent than ever, as evidenced by the success of touring advocacy groups such as the Adventure Cycling Association and the proliferation of cycle touring companies offering supported tours in scenic locales. The mood now is not so different from the 1880s: regular folks are discovering, or at least considering, the possibilities of cycling, as a means to take an active (and relatively guilt-free) vacation. In this sense, the general message of "those Pennells"—that cycling is "the most delightful manner of getting about and seeing a country, of taking a holiday"[63]—still speaks to many readers today.

# A Note on the Text

THIS EDITION IS BASED ON Seeley and Company's first English editions of the two works. In the case of *An Italian Pilgrimage*, however, I have chosen to omit the final two chapters of the English edition, neither of which is about the Pennells' ride from Florence to Rome. The first one, "The Stones of Rome," the title of which is a play off of John Ruskin's three-volume *The Stones of Venice* (1851–1853), first appeared in Philip Gilbert Hamerton's *Portfolio* (London: Seeley, 1885, pp. 158–72). It is a guided tour of some of the highlights of Rome's art and architecture. The second one, "Vetturino *versus* Tricycle," by Joseph, appeared in *Outing* 6.2 (May 1885), pp. 230–32, and offers a side-by-side comparison of the routes taken by Nathaniel Hawthorne, who travelled from Rome to Florence in 1858 with his family, and the Pennells in 1884. These two chapters were included in the English edition only after the publisher, Seeley, insisted that the Pennells' original manuscript was too short. In response to Seeley, Elizabeth proposed adding her "Stones of Rome" piece, which was written the winter following their cycle trip while the Pennells stayed over in Rome. At first, Joseph objected to the inclusion of these two chapters, seeing the addition as an obvious attempt to "pad the book," but he eventually gave in to Seeley's request and offered the short "Vetturino" piece (*LL1*: 181).

An Italian Pilgrimage was published in a slightly different version in the United States around the same time by Roberts Brothers under the title *Two Pilgrims' Progress*. Although this American version lacked the supplementary chapters mentioned above and includes two fewer illustrations than the English one, it did feature added chapter epigraphs from Bunyan's *Pilgrims Progress*, an extra section in the prefatory poem by Leland, and some minor changes to punctuation and translation of foreign words. Although Elizabeth explains in her *Life and Letters of Joseph Pennell* that *Two Pilgrims' Progress* was, in fact, their original title for the work, she seemed unhappy, in general, with the American edition (*LL1*: 187). She preferred Seeley's English version, in part, because she felt that Seeley "took pride in the appearance of his books." The cover of the American version was so "glaring" that it "made us long to suppress it," she wrote (187). I have chosen to base this new edition on the English one, believing that the Pennells themselves liked it better.

I have standardized some of the punctuation but maintained Elizabeth Robins Pennell's somewhat eccentric use of italics.

D.B.

# A Canterbury Pilgrimage

RIDDEN, WRITTEN, AND ILLUSTRATED BY
JOSEPH & ELIZABETH ROBINS PENNELL.

TO

Mr. Robert Louis Stevenson,[1]

*We, who are unknown to him,*
*dedicate this record of one of our short*
*journeys on a Tricycle,*
*in gratitude for the happy hours we have spent*
*travelling with him and his Donkey.*

We do not think our book needs an apology, explanation, or preface; nor does it seem to us worth while to give our route-form, since the road from London to Canterbury is almost as well known to cyclers as the Strand, or the Lancaster Pike;[2] nor to record our time, since we were pilgrims and not scorchers. And as for non-cyclers, who as yet know nothing of time and roads, we would rather show them how pleasant it is to go on pilgrimage than weary them with cycling facts.

Joseph Pennell.
Elizabeth Robins Pennell.

36 Bedford Place,
May 14th, 1885.

# | A Canterbury Pilgrimage

IT WAS TOWARDS THE END OF AUGUST, when a hot sun was softening the asphalt in the dusty streets of London, and ripening the hops in the pleasant land of Kent, that we went on pilgrimage to Canterbury.[3] Ours was no ordinary journey by rail, which is the way latter-day pilgrims mostly travel. No. What we wanted was in all reverence to follow, as far as it was possible, the road taken by the famous company of bygone days, setting out from the hostelrie where these lordings lay one night and held counsel, making stations by the way at the few places they mention by name, and ending it, as they did, at the shrine of the 'holy, blissful martyr,' in the Canterbury Cathedral. How better could this be done than by riding over the ground made sacred by them on our tricycle?

*Pilgrims new and old.*

*Our only Race.*

And so it came to pass that one close, foggy morning, we strapped our bags to our machine and wheeled out of Russell Square before any one was stirring but the policeman, making his last rounds and trying door after door. Down Holborn and past Staples' Inn, very grey and venerable in the pale light, and where the facetious driver of a donkey-cart tried to race us; past the now silent and deserted cloisters of Christ's Hospital, and under Bow Bells in Cheapside; past the monument of the famous fire, and over London Bridge, where the mist was heavy on the river and the barges showed spectre-like through it, and where hucksters greeted us after their fashion, one crying, "Go in, hind one! I bet on you. You'll catch up if you try hard enough!" and another, "How are you there, up in the second story?" A short way up the Borough High Street, from which we had a glimpse of the old red roof and

*Tricycle vs. horse.*

balustraded galleries of the "White Hart;" and then we were at the corner where the "Tabard"[4] ought to be. This was to have been our starting-point; but how, it suddenly occurred to us for the first time, could we start from nothing? If ours had no beginning, would it be a genuine pilgrimage? This was a serious difficulty at the very outset. But our enthusiasm was fresh. We looked up at the old sign of *"Ye Old Tabard,"* hanging from the third story of the tall brick building which has replaced Chaucer's Inn. Here, at least, was something substantial. And we rode on with what good cheer we could.

Then we went for some distance over the Old Kent Road, which is laid with Belgian paving[5]—invented, I think, for the confusion of cyclers, and where in one place a Hansom cab blocked the way. In endeavouring to pass around it our big wheel ran into the groove of the track, and we had to

*The Pilgrims are Chased by Dogs.*

dismount and lift it out. The driver sat scowling as he looked on. If he had
his way, he said, he would burn all *them things*. We came to Deptford, or West
Greenwich, at half-past seven, the very hour when mine host and his fellows
passed.[6] So, in remembrance of them, we stopped a few minutes opposite
a little street full of old two-storied houses, with tiled roofs and clustered
chimney-pots and casement windows, overtopped by a distant church steeple,
its outline softened in the silvery mist, for the fog was growing less as we jour-
neyed onwards. At the corner was an Inn called the "Fountain," and as a man
who talked with us while we rested there said that an old fountain had stood
in the open space near by, it pleased us to think that here had been one of the
Waterings of Saint Thomas[7] where pilgrims to the shrine made short halts, and
that perhaps it was at this very spot that Davy Copperfield,[8] a modern pilgrim
who travelled the same road, had come to a stop in his flight from the young
man with a donkey-cart. A little way out of Deptford we came to Blackheath,
where sheep were peacefully grazing, rooks cawing overhead, and two or three
bicyclers racing, and where a woman stopped us to say that "That's the 'ouse of
Prince Harthur yander, and onst the Princess Sophia[9] stayed in it on her way to
Woolwich," and she pointed to the handsome brick house to our left.

After Blackheath the mist vanished, and the sun, gladdened by the sweet
air, shone on the fields and woods, and the ugly barracks and pretty cottages by
which we wheeled. Red-coated soldiers turned to look and dogs ran out to bark
at us. In the meadows men and women leaned on their hoes and rakes to stare.

*An Enterprising Pilgrim.*

From tiny gardens, overflowing with roses and sunflowers, children waved their delight. London was many miles behind when, at a few minutes before nine, we drew up on the bridge at Crayford.

It seemed at first a sleepy little village. The only signs of life were on the bridge. Here about a dozen men were smoking their morning pipes, and as many boys were leaning over the wall, lazily staring into the river below, or at the cool stretches of woodland and shady orchards on the hillside beyond. But presently, as we waited, the village clock struck nine, and at once the loud bell in the factory on the other side of the little river Cray began to ring. One by one the older loungers knocked the ashes from their pipes and passed through the gate. The boys lingered. But their evil genius, in the shape of an old man in a tall white cap, came out, and at his bidding they left the sunshine and the river and hurried to work. A man with a cart full of shining onions went by, and we followed him up a hilly street, where the gabled and timbered cottages seemed to be trying to climb one over the other to reach a terrace of shining white houses at the top. The first of these was but one-storied, and its tall chimney-pot threw a soft blue shadow on the higher wall of the house next to it. On a short strip of ground which stretched along the terrace patches of cabbages alternated with luxuriant crops of weeds. In one place there were stalks of pink hollyhock and poles covered with vines, and in the windows above were scarlet geraniums. About them all there was a feeling of warmth and light, more like Italy than England. J. took out his sketch-book. Several

*An Indifferent Pilgrim.*

women, startled by the novelty of strangers passing by, had come out and were standing in their small gardens. When they saw the sketch-book they posed as if for a photographer—all except one old woman, who hobbled down the street, talking glibly. Perhaps it was as well we did not hear what she said, for I think she was cursing us. When she was close at our side and turned, waving her hands to the other women, she looked like a great bird of ill-omen. "Go in! go in!" she croaked: "he's takin' of yere likenesses. That's wot he's arter!" Her wrath still fell upon us as we wheeled out of Crayford.

There were many pilgrims on the road; a few, like us, were on machines, but the greater number were on foot. As in Chaucer's day, both rich and poor go upon pilgrimage through Kent; but, whereas in his time there were monasteries and hospitals by the way where the latter were taken in at night, now they must find shelter under hedges or in dingles.[10] Their lot, however, did not seem hard. It is sweet to lie beneath the sky now as it was when Daphnis sang.[11] And the pilgrims whom we saw looked as if soft turf was luxury compared to the beds they had just left, for they belonged to the large army of hop-pickers who, every autumn, come from London to make the Kentish roads unsafe after dark and the householder doubly watchful. Whitechapel and other low quarters are nearly emptied at this season. It is pleasant to know that at least once a-year these people escape from their smoky, squalid streets, into green places where they can breathe pure air, but their coming is not welcomed in the country.

*Crayford.*

Many poor, honest women in towns and villages thereabouts will rather lose a few shillings than let their children go to the hop-fields during the picking season, lest they should come away but too much wiser than they went. As we rode further the number of tramps increased; all the morning we passed and overtook them. There were grey-haired, decrepit men and women, who hobbled painfully along, and could scarcely keep pace with their more stalwart sons and daughters; there were children by the score, some of whom ran gaily on, forgetting fatigue for joy of the sunshine; others lagged behind, whimpering and weary; and still others were borne in their mothers' arms. Almost all these people were laden with their household goods and gods. They carried heavy bags thrown over their shoulders, or else baskets and bundles slung on their arms, and pots and kettles and all manner of household furniture. One man, more enterprising than the others, had brought a push-cart; when we saw it, two babies, almost hidden in a confused mass of clothing and pots and pans, were sleeping in it, and one clasped a kitten in her arms. Now, with a sharp bend in the road, we came suddenly upon a man sitting under a tree, who, though we rang our bell right in his ear, never raised his eyes from a hole in an old silk handkerchief he was holding; and now we came to a man and woman resting on a pile of stones by the roadside, who sat upright at the tinkling of our bell. I shall never forget the red and swarthy face of the woman as she turned and looked at us, her black hair, coarse and straight as an Indian's, hanging about her shoulders and over her eyes: she was unmistakably

*Unwelcome Pilgrims.*

young in years but old in vice, and ignorant of all save evil—compared to hers an idiot's face would have been intelligent, a brute's refined. I could now understand why honest countrywomen kept their children from the hop-fields. As a rule, the tramps were as careless and jolly as Béranger's Bohemians,[12] and laughed and made merry as if the world and its hardships were but jests. We, as figures in the farce, came in for a share of their mirth. "That's right! ladies fust!" one old tattered and torn man called after us, gaily; "that's the principle on which I allus hacts!" Which, I suppose, is a rough way of saying "*Place aux dames.*" A very little joke went a great way with them. "Clear the path!" another man cried to the women walking with him, as we coasted down the hill outside of Dartford: "'ere's a lady and gen'leman on a happaratus a-runnin' over us!" "They're only a 'enjoyin' of 'emselves," an old hag of the party added; "so let luck go wi' 'em!" Then she laughed loud and long, and the others joined with her, and the sound of their laughter still reached our ears as we came into the village.

Dartford, from a cycler's point of view, is a long narrow street between two hills, one of which is good to coast, the other hard to climb. The place, as we saw it, was full of hucksters and waggons, and footmen and carriages, and we passed on without stopping, save by the river that runs near a church, with a tower and an unconventional clock looking out from one side instead of from the centre, which is the proper place for clocks.

From Dartford to Gravesend the road became more pleasant every minute. Here and there were brown fields, where men were ploughing, or

*Uphill Grind.*

perhaps burning heaps of stubble, and sending pale grey clouds of smoke
heavenwards; here and there were golden meadows where gleaners were busy,
and then, perhaps, a row of tall, dark poplars, or a patch of brilliant cabbages.
To the south, broad plains, where lazy, ease-loving cattle were grazing,
stretched as far as the eye could see. To the north, every now and then, as the
road turned, we saw the river, where ships were at anchor, and steamers were
steaming up to London, and black barges, with dark-red sails, were floating
down with the tide. The water was blue as the sky, and the hills in the distance
seemed to melt into a soft purple mist hanging over them. By the road and by
the river were many deep deserted quarries, whose white chalk cliffs could be
seen from afar, while they brought out in strong contrast the red roofs of the
cottages built at their feet. We came to one or two small villages and another
church, with its tower and a clock awry, so that we wondered whether this was
a fashion in Kent. And all along the hedges were white and pink with open
morning-glories, and the trees threw soft shadows over the white road, and
everywhere the air was sweet with the scent of clematis.

Gravesend is not a very striking place as you enter it from the road. It
was to us remarkable chiefly for the Rosherville Gardens, which hitherto we
had known only in our Dickens.[13] But we found a pleasant "ale-stake" by the
river, where we rested to "both drinke and biten on a cake;"[14] or, rather, on
substantial beefsteak and vegetables. There was no one else in the coffee-room,
but one or two dogs strayed in from the private bar, and seeing we were at

*Burning Stubble near Gravesend.*

dinner became very sociable. The maid who waited on us was friendly too, and while J. was busy putting away the tricycle she was even moved to confide in me. She was the only maid in the house, she said. There had been another, but she had gone some time ago; "and there's a jolly hard lot of work for one woman to do, ma'am," she went on. "I'm not used to it, and I can't stand it much longer. I've always been in a private before. It's easy enough to go from a private to a public, but to get from a public to a private again is another thing. Onst in a public is always in a public, ma'am!" Then some one called her. I was glad to have her go, for her way of telling her trouble had in it something of the Greek doctrine of fate, and so long as her eye was upon me I had an uncomfortable feeling, as if I were one of the instruments decreed from all time to work out her cheerless destiny. It was more agreeable to look out of the window on the little lawn in front, where two comfortable matrons were drinking beer, and a Blue-coat boy, home for the holidays, was running around, showing his orange legs to the best advantage. It was quiet on the river. Large steamers, small steam-tugs and row-boats, were lying at anchor. An old coastguard hulk was moored opposite, and an officer walked solemnly up and down the deck, every now and then halting to look through a spyglass for suspicious craft. But as we stood on the pier, after we had dined, the tide turned, and swiftly and silently all the boats turned with it. Tugs gave shrill whistles in warning of their speedy departure. Sail-boats unfurled their sails. Sailors came down the watersteps, leading from the houses built on high walls at the water's edge,

*By the River at Gravesend.*

and rowed quickly to the coastguard boat, saluted the solitary officer, and disappeared below. In the large P. and O. steamer,[15] anchored at some distance from the pier, we could see the red turbans and white tunics of Lascars moving to and fro on the decks. The river was now as lively as it had before been quiet. But it monopolised the activity of the place, for when we went back for our tricycle we met only one or two seamen and a handful of children.

When we set forth again the air was warm and sleep-inspiring. This, together with the consciousness of having well dined, it must be confessed, made us return to the pedals unwillingly. Not even the fact that a whole Sunday school, off for a picnic, waited to look at us, could stimulate us into speed. A sun-dial on a church tower just outside of Gravesend seemed to take us to task for our indolence. In large black letters on its white face it said—

"Be quick: your time's short!"

But we knew better. Rochester was but seven miles off, and in Rochester we had made up our minds to sleep that night. The tramps had grown as lazy as we, but they did not even pretend to struggle with their laziness. All along the road we saw them lying under the hedges and in shady places. Some were asleep, others day-dreaming. Three women had roused themselves somewhat, and were making preparations for afternoon tea. They had kindled a fire by the wayside, and hung their kettle over it. A little further on, a mother and her

*Afternoon Tea.*

children were just coming to the road from the deep, sweet shade of a dingle. On the hill beyond was a grey church, with a graveyard whose graves straggled down the hillside, and next to it a large farmhouse, with red roof and walls, whose colour was softened and harmonised by time. When the children saw we had stopped the machine they ran up at once to beg us to buy queer little round calico-balls, which they called pin-cushions. One had bright black eyes, and, not in the least discomfited by our refusal of the balls, danced merrily around the tricycle. Then she peered into J.'s sketch-book.

"He's drawrin!" she called to her mother, in a loud stage whisper.

The latter bade her mind her manners. But she still continued her observations.

"Oh, mother, it's the church!" was her next cry.

"Which, I'm sure, it's a werry decent church," the mother declared, as if to encourage us with her approval; and then they went their way.

Later, when, as we were coasting down a hill, we overtook the party, the same child jumped and clapped her hands, "It's goin' all by its lone self!" she screamed; but her sister trudged stolidly on, and spake never a word.

Of the many places on the road to Canterbury, made famous by latter-day ·pilgrims, few are better known and loved than Gad's Hill, where honest Jack Falstaff performed his deeds of valour,[16] and where Charles Dickens spent the last years of his life.[17] We had counted upon making it, too, a station by the way. But whether it was that we were just then drifting along in lotus-eaters' fashion, our feet moving mechanically, or whether the prospect of another long coast made us forgetful of all else, certain it is that, with a glance of admiration at the dark spreading cedars, and another at the inn and its sign, adorned with the picture of Falstaff, we went by without a thought as to where we were. At the foot of the hill a baker told us that up yonder was the house where Mr. Dickens had lived. Were we already in danger of forgetting the aim of our pilgrimage? Would we sacrifice our great end for what we had intended to be but a means to it? "Let us," I said humbly, "try to keep our wits from wool-gathering again, lest we ride through Rochester and Canterbury without knowing it!" We collected our thoughts in good time; for, lo! as mine host said to the monk, Rochester stands there hard by. Before many minutes we saw in the distance the town of Strood, and beyond it the broad Medway and Rochester, its castle and cathedral towering above the houses clustering about them.

We stayed all night in Rochester. The early pilgrims went to the "Crown." But the "Crown," alas! stands no longer, and so we slept at the "Queen's Head," the C.T.C. headquarters.[18] There is, somewhere in the city, the chapel where pious travellers of old stopped to pray, but we could not find it. The further we went the more it seemed as if we were in pursuit of a shadow. And, indeed, it was here that we discovered that even the road we had ridden over was not that along which mine host and his company had passed as they told their tales. There was no use, however, in our going back to London and starting out again, so as to take the right road; for, alas! it—that is, as far as Rochester—has gone the way of the Tabard and Crown. Only the yew-trees, planted at intervals along its course, survive to show where it once ran.

After we had had our tea, we walked out in the twilight. The town deserves the name of Dulborough,[19] given it by Dickens; and so, indeed, our little maid at the inn thought. There was nothing to do to amuse one's self, she said. She had been up to London for a month in the spring, and since then she couldn't abide Rochester.

Having produced a Castle and ruined it, and a Cathedral and restored it, it has ever since rested on its laurels. We wandered a little way through the narrow twisting street, meeting only soldiers and a few young girls and men, and through the gabled gatehouse, where opium-eating Jasper lived;[20] past the wonderful Norman doorway of the Cathedral and then to the Castle, where we rested awhile in the public garden the city has made around it. The pigeons had gone to roost, two or three women sat silently on the benches, a group of children played a singing game in the Pavilion. Away in the west, beyond the river, we could see the green and yellow fields and the poplars, radiant in the light of the afterglow; on the horizon, a dark windmill rose above the hillside like a sentinel on duty, and its long arms moved slowly around. It was even more peaceful down by the river: two men were pulling a long outrigger against the tide; a few heavy-laden barges floated up the stream with it. The figures of the men on board were silhouetted in black against the now fading western light. The red sails were furled and the masts slowly fell as the barges neared the bridge; noiselessly and swiftly they disappeared under the black arches. They seemed to carry with them all the sounds of the day; the silence of night came over the place, our voices sank lower, and we walked quietly back to the lonely street and to the Inn.

## Second Day

There was a little more stir in the place the next morning, but it was because it was filled with tramps, who were wisely taking advantage of the early coolness and hurrying on their way. But when we turned off the High Street the town was as still in the glare of day as it had been in the late twilight. The high brick walls of the private gardens might have enclosed dwelling-places of the dead rather than of the living, for not a sound came over them. The little pointed houses might have been sepulchers for all the signs of life they gave. The whole town, instead of one little street, should be called Tranquil Place. It seemed very characteristic that the Cathedral should be closed, and this at the season when the tourist is abroad in the land. It was being cleaned, an old man told us. We looked through the iron railing of the door into the nave, and at the marble floor, and the tall, white, rounded arches. "It's like looking down the throat of Old Time!" Mr. Grewgious thought when he stood there.[21] At the farther end by the chancel steps a charwoman was at work on bended knees.

By her side was one small bucket. Here, truly, was a Liliputian set to do the work of Brobdignag.[22] At that rate it is probable visitors were shut out for many months.

After we had looked at the "Bull," which still reminds the public by a sign of the good beds enjoyed by Mr. Pickwick and his friends,[23] at the Town Hall where Pip was apprenticed, at the many-gabled, lattice-windowed house in which Rosa Bud bloomed into young ladyhood, and were standing in front of the "Six Poor Travellers" lodging-place, reading the inscription over the door, and wondering who were the proctors classed with rogues who could not rest within, a benevolent Englishman passing that way fell upon us. He was a worthy fellow-citizen of Richard Watts. Seeing we were strangers, he, without waiting to be asked, bestowed upon us the charity of information.

"Do you know what a Proctor is, Sir?" he asked, addressing himself to J., who meekly, as befits one receiving alms, said that he did not. "No! Well, then, I will tell you. It is a proc-u-ra-tor,—one who collects Peter's pence for the Pope, Sir. Richard Watts lived in the sixteenth century, when Protestantism made people feel bitterly, Sir, and he would have no friends of the Pope beneath his roof. Proc-u-ra-tor! That's what a Proctor is, Sir."

He had disappeared around the curve of the street before we had finished thanking him. As the information was new to us, I, with the common belief that others must be as ignorant as myself, now imitate his benevolence, and here bestow it in alms upon whoever may be in need of it.

It was one o'clock when we mounted our tricycle and set out once more for Canterbury. The sky was still unclouded and the day warm, but a good breeze was blowing, and we were fresh for our ride. The streets of Chatham were as busy as those of Rochester were idle, and blocked with waggons, so that we had to fall in line and go at snail's pace. Once, with a sudden halt, we were brought so near a horse just in front, that my foot knocked against his leg; but he bore the blow stoically, as if he were used to Chatham streets. An American circus was about to start out on its grand street parade, and children hung about corners and out of windows. At the foot of the hill outside the town, and marked "Dangerous" by the National Cyclists' Union,[24] for the benefit of cyclers, two very small boys offered to "Push it up, Sir!" but as it looked as if *it* would push them down, we declined. At the top we met a cycler on his way from Canterbury, and he gave us evil tidings of the road. It became worse with every mile, he said, and it was heavy and hilly, and the dust was enough to stifle one. To this last statement his appearance bore good testimony.

*The Marshes.*

But at first we found it fair enough. From Chatham to Sittingbourne our journey was one of unmixed pleasure. The wheels went easily, and the wind blew on our backs. Now we passed on our right a vast treeless expanse, divided into squares of green, and golden, and brown, all shining softly in the sunlight, with here and there a windmill; but to the left we could see far below us the white line of the river winding between the flat grey marshes, where in Pip's day the escaped convicts prowled. Again we wheeled through small, sleepy villages, with church and tower half hidden in clumps of trees, and with red oasts, whose crooked cowls loomed up over the chimney-pots of the low cottages: for we had come to the hop country, and at every step the land of Kent grew fairer. Beyond Rainham the road lay between hop-gardens, as they are appropriately called, and cherry-orchards. In places the vines formed tall, shady hedges; in others the gardens were shut in by bare poles hung with coarse brown cloth, to defy the wind and the depredations of small boys, and other destructive animals: but the prettiest fields were those which were in no way hedged about, so that we could look down the long, narrow, green aisles, which seemed to lead to fields of light beyond. The vines twisted lovingly up the poles, which in many places bent beneath masses of green fruit, or else the topmost shoots crossed and intertwined from one pole to another, and the whole field was woven into a large arbour. Where the sunlight fell upon the

*A Cherry Orchard.*

green clusters it turned them to pure gold, and the leaves, blowing gently to and fro, seemed to rejoice in their great beauty. The cherry-orchards were so pretty and trim that I wondered if, like the hop-fields, they were not sometimes called gardens. The trees had been long stripped of their fruit, but their branches were well covered with cool green leaves, and their shadows met on the grass beneath. There was one in particular, before which we rested. Sheep were browsing placidly on the downy turf, and when we looked low down between the trees we could see the shining white river far in the distance. I half expected to hear a new Daphnis and Menalcas singing their pastorals in gentle rivalry.[25]

We met few people. The tramps who come down to Kent for the hop-picking turn off from Rochester to go to Maidstone, where the largest hop-fields are, and where there is more chance for them to be hired; but a comparatively small number go on to Canterbury. Some cyclers were making the most of the fine day. As we sat idly between the hop-gardens three passed us. Two rode a tandem; the third, a bicycle; but they were of the time-making species, for whom the only beauty of a ride is that of speed. Looking at them, and then at the sheep in a field beyond, I thought the latter were having the best of it. A little further on we met a party of three Frenchmen. One rode ahead on a bicycle, the two others followed on a tandem like ours. One of the

*A Kentish Pastoral.*

latter, when he saw us, called out to the bicycler, *"C'est bon d'aller comme ça!"*[26] I suppose he thought we should not understand him, and if we did—well, ought not a Frenchman always to be gallant?

We rode on with light hearts. An eternity of wheeling through such perfect country and in such soft sunshine would, we thought, be the true earthly paradise. We were at peace with ourselves and with all mankind, and J. even went so far as to tell me I had never ridden so well!

It was, then, in a happy frame of mind, that we reached the inn at Sittingbourne. It was an unassuming place, but quiet and clean; the bar was on one side of the hall, the coffee-room on the other. The latter was empty, and the landlady, after laying the cloth for our bread and cheese and shandy-gaff—of all drinks the most refreshing to the cycler—left us alone to study this printed notice, which hung in a frame over the door:—

"Call frequently,
Drink moderately,
Pay honourably,
Be good company,
Part friendly,
Go home quietly."

We soon had the opportunity of putting into practice one clause of this advice, for the door was suddenly burst open, and a short man with a bald head, who wore the Cyclists' Touring Club uniform, rushed in.

"Are you the lady and gentleman that came on the tandem?" he asked, before he was quite in the room.

We said we were.

"I don't like tandems, do you?" he continued, fiercely, as if he were daring us to differ from him. He seemed to think we had come there that he might tell us his grievances; which he did, with much elaboration, while we ate our lunch. He and his wife had been down to Margate from London, and were now on their way back, he said. They had made the trip on a tandem; it was the first time he had ridden one, and it would be the last, for he didn't like tandems—they were horrid things! Did we like tandems? To avoid repetition, I may here mention that this expression of dislike, together with the query as to our opinion, was the refrain to everything he said. It was always given with the same interest and emphasis as if it were an entirely original remark. The only variation he made was by sometimes beginning with the statement, and at others with the question. He explained the reasons for his dislike. The principal was, that the people one met on the roads always insulted riders on a tandem. Why, he had been off his machine a dozen times that morning, fighting men who had been chaffing him! I thought, with a shudder, of the crowd of hucksters J. would have had to fight by London Bridge, had he been of the same mind. Then, the next objection was, that he had to sit behind his wife—she had to steer, and he would not be surprised if he were seriously injured, or even killed, before he got back to London. Women were heedless things, and easily frightened. His wife, who had joined us a few minutes before, here grew angry, and a slight skirmish of words followed between them: she reminded him of the dangers they had escaped through her nerve and skill; he recalled the dangers into which they had run owing to her thoughtlessness and timidity. But, just at this point of the discussion J. took out his watch. At sight of it the little man forgot his anger to pounce upon it, with never as much as "An it please you!" Then, looking up in triumph, he exclaimed, "I knew it! it's an American watch! They know how to make watches over there, but they're ruining our trade." Then he explained that he was a London watchmaker, and he pulled out of his pocket a large substantial specimen of his workmanship.

The talk now turning upon America, we told him, in answer to his inquiries, that we were Americans.

*Scorchers.*

"From Canada?" his wife asked.

"Oh, no!" I answered; "from Philadelphia."

"Dear me!" the watchmaker said; "then you're *real* Americans! But you speak English very well!"

"Yes," J. admitted, modestly. "But then, you know, English is sometimes spoken in our part of the world!"

All this made the fierce little cycler very friendly, and he next wanted to know where we were going.

"To Canterbury," we said.

"To Canterbury!" he cried; and then, to give greater force to his words, he came and stood directly in front of us on the other side of the table. "To Canterbury! Well, then, my advice to you is, if you have no other object than pleasure, don't go! No, don't you go! I've been there, and I know what I say. It's a rotten place. There's nothing in it but an old cathedral and a lot of old houses and churches, and they charged me sixpence for keeping my tandem one night. I don't like tandems—horrid things! Do you like tandems? Yes, it's a rotten place, and if I had my way I'd raze it to the ground!"

I now understand why it is that Mr. Matthew Arnold thinks the average Briton so very terrible.[27]

By this time we had finished our lunch, and were ready to start. The watchmaker and his wife had engaged in another battle. She did not agree with him in his opinion of Canterbury. Indeed I believe they did not agree upon any one subject, and the tandem had tried their tempers. They had both said they wanted to see us off, and to compare machines; but we, being modest people, thought we would as lieve escape without their comments and farewells. This seemed a favourable opportunity. In the heat of the argument we left the room and paid our bill, without their noticing our retreat; but just as we had mounted our tricycle, and were wheeling softly away, we heard a voice calling, "Oh, I say now! do come back a minute: I want to show you my machine!" It would have been more than uncivil to have refused, so we sat patiently while the much-abused tandem was brought out. The owner, in his pride, rode out on it, pedalled by us, and then wheeled round and faced us with an abruptness that fairly took away our breath. It was the shortest turn I have ever seen, and I waited for the end with the same uncertainty with which one watches a trapeze performance. Then there was some little talk about bells and brakes, and tyres and saddles. In the meantime the landlady, with two or three of her friends, had come out, and was staring at us with a curiosity for which I could not account. But presently

*A Farmhouse near Rochester.*

she said, "Are you going back soon?" And then I knew she had heard we were Americans, and had come to have a look at these strange people who had sailed across the sea, apparently for no other reason than to test the cycling properties of the roads of Kent. After this exhibition was over we said good-bye very pleasantly, and rode off, followed by their wishes for our good luck, while the watchmaker called out encouragingly, "You Americans ride pretty well; but I don't like tandems. Horrid things! Do you like tandems?"

But their wishes were the only good luck we met with. We had not gone far from Sittingbourne, when we admitted that the pilgrim we had met just outside of Chatham was no false prophet after all; for the road now began to be heavy with sand and rough with flints. And oh, the hills! They were not very steep, but I was a novice in cycling. No sooner were we on up-grades than I exhausted myself by my vigorous back-pedalling.[28] I have heard the uninitiated say that tricycling must be so easy, just like working the velocipedes of our childhood. But let them try! The country had lost none of its beauty. Fields were as green and golden, orchards as shady, and sheep as peaceful, as those we had seen before lunch. There were little churches on hilltops and pretty dingles by the wayside; handsome country-houses with well-kept lawns, and fields where cricketers were playing, and young girls in gay-coloured dresses were applauding; and there were old-fashioned farm-houses and quaint inn-yards. We passed through villages by which little quiet rivers ran, some with boats lying by the shore, and others, as at Ospringe, where horses and waggons were calmly driven through the water. But the heaviness had spread from the road to my heart, and all joyousness had gone from me.

*A Little River.*

The worst of it was, that as the road here wound little, we could see it miles ahead—a white perpendicular line on the purple hill which bounded the horizon. We knew this must be Boughton Hill, the fame of whose steepness has gone abroad in the cycling world. With the knowledge of what was to come ever before me, I began to pedal so badly that J. told me so very plainly, and said, moreover, that I was more of a hindrance than a help to him. For some time we rode on very silently. Earlier in the afternoon we had been passed by a man driving an empty carriage, of whom we had asked one or two questions. He had stopped to watch the cricket-match, but he now overtook us, and, to add to my misery, asked me if I would not like him to drive me into Canterbury. All this was hard to bear.

Finally, we came to Boughton,[29] a small village with ivy-grown houses and a squirrel and a dolphin staring at each other amicably from rival inns. It is right at the foot of Boughton Hill. Now that we were near it, the white line we had seen for so long widened into a broad road, but it looked no less perpendicular. It was here that Chaucer's pilgrims

"gan atake[30]
A man that clothed was in clothes blake,
And undernethe he wered a white surplis."

*Archway.*

There is no record that mine host and the Chanones Yeman dismounted and walked to rest their horses. But all the many waggons and carriages and cycles we saw above us on the modern road were being led, not driven. Halfway up was an old lumbering stage, with boxes piled on the top, and big baskets and bundles swinging underneath. The driver was walking; but a tramp, who had made believe to push when on level ground, now sat comfortably on the backseat, taking his ease. A little lower was the friendly driver with his empty carriage, for he had rested at the "Squirrel," and so we had caught up to him again. At the top we looked back to see that the West was a broad sea of shining light. A yellow mist hung over the plain, softening and blending its many colours. Far off to the north the river glittered and sparkled, and a warm glow spread over the green of the near hillsides. The way in front of us was grey and colourless by comparison. It was almost all down-hill after this. Did I want to be driven into Canterbury, indeed? My benevolent friend might now have asked us to pull him in. The stage made a show of racing us, but we gave it only a minute's chance. An officer in braided coat driving a drag passed us triumphantly while we were on our up-grade; but when we came again to a level we left him far behind.

*Canterbury Cathedral.*

"Wete ye not wher stondeth a litel toun,
Which that ycleped is Bob up-and-doun,
Under the blee in Canterbury way?"[31]

It is better known now as Harbledown. A little of our trouble here came back, for the road leading to that part of it 'ycleped Bob-up,' was steep and heavy, and we had to walk. To our right were the old red-brick almshouses and the little church of St. Michael, one of the many oldest churches in Kent, and of which all we could see was the ivy-covered tower. It was here that Henry, when on his way to the holy shrine, dismounted, that, as became his humble calling of pilgrim, he might walk into Canterbury. And it was here, too, that the Person began his long-winded discourse. But we, less reverent than King Henry, now mounted again; and, less phlegmatic than the Person, we held our peace. For as we rode further up we heard far-away chimes, just as Erasmus did when he went from Harbledown;[32] and there gradually rose before us a tall, grey tower, then two more, and at last, as we reached the top of the hill, we saw in the plain below the great Cathedral itself, standing up far above the low red roofs of Canterbury. We were almost at our goal.

A little further on we passed a hop-field, where the picking had already begun. In one part the poles were stripped of their vines, so that it looked as if the farmer had reaped for his sowing a crop of dead sticks. In the other the

*Women with Baskets.*

poles were still green, but the day's work was just over. Women were packing up kettles and pans, jugs and bottles, and stowing babies and bundles into perambulators, while two or three men were going the rounds with bag and basket, measuring the day's picking, and marking off the account of each picker by notching short, flat pieces of wood held up for the purpose. In the road beyond a large cart, packed with well-filled bags, was being drawn homewards by three horses, while a young man rode up and down the green aisles. "I beg your pardon, Sir," a farm hand said to J., who had been sketching, "but you've been takin' some of our people, and now you hought to take our Guvnor on his 'oss;" and he pointed to the young man. All the way into the town we passed groups of pickers: women with large families of children, small boys with jugs and coats hung over their shoulders, and young girls with garlands of hops twisted about their hats, and all were as merry as if they had been on a picnic. We saw them still before us, even after we had turned into Saint Dunstan's Street, from which the gold of the afterglow was fast fading, and were riding between the quaint, gabled houses, through whose diamond-paned windows lights were beginning to appear. Before us was the old, grey-towered city gate, through which royal and ecclesiastical processions and knights and nobles once passed, but where we now saw only the tramps who had arrived at the eleventh hour sitting at its foot with their bags and baggage.

*Westgate.*

We "toke" our inn at the sign of the "Falstaff," without the gate. Honest Jack, in buff doublet and red hose, hanging between the projecting windows and far out over the pavement by a wonderful piece of wrought-iron work, gave us welcome, and within we found rest and good cheer for weary pilgrims. Then we "ordeyned" our dinner wisely, but it was too late to go to the Cathedral that same evening, as we should have liked to have done, and we were forced to wait for the morrow. After we had come downstairs from our dimity-curtained bed-chamber, had dined, and were sitting over our tea in a little, low-ceilinged room, from whose window we looked into a pretty garden of roses and grape-vines, a stranger sent us greeting, and asked if he might come and sit with us. He was a priest, also making pilgrimage, who had ridden from Rochester on a machine like ours; so that we became friendly forthwith, and, like the pilgrims who rested at the "Chequers of the Hope," every man of our party

> "in his wyse made hertly chere,
> Telling his felowe of sportys and of chere,
> And of other mirthis that fellen by the way,
> As custom is of pilgrims and hath been many a day."

And just before we parted for the night we held counsel together and agreed that, in the morning, we would in company visit the holy shrine.

### Third Day

We rose early the next day, and, that we might be
in all possible things like the men in whose steps
we were walking, we "cast on fresher gowns" before
we started to walk through the town. Then, after
we had breakfasted, we set out with our new friend
for the Cathedral. Our way led through the gate, on
which the sun shone brightly, and where tramps
were still waiting to be hired; and then through the
High Street, filled with other pilgrims, who spake
divers tongues, who wore not sandal, but canvas
shoon, and who had their "signys" in their hands
and upon their "capps," for many had puggarees
about their hats, and still more carried red guide-
books. The air was warm, but fresh and pure as if
the sea-breeze had touched it; and the gables and carvings of the old houses
were glowing with sunlight. The reflection of the red roofs and of geraniums
and hollyhocks in gardens by the way made bright bits of colour in among
the tall reeds of the little river Stour, and as we went slowly along we talked,
as befitted the occasion, of bygone times, for at every step we were reminded
of those earlier travellers whose humble followers we were. Here we came to

*Waiting to be Hired.*

the Hospital of St. Thomas, now an almshouse, of old the place where poor pilgrims found shelter; and here, in the ground-floor of a haberdasher's shop, we saw a few arches of what was once the "Chequers of the Hope," where the rich were lodged; and so, when in Mercery Lane, where the houses almost met above in a friendly, confidential way, we saw a man in cocked-hat and knee-breeches and much gold lace, it seemed as if he, like everything else in Canterbury, must be a relic of the olden time.

"I must know who that fellow is!" the priest exclaimed; and, without more ado, walked up to him and boldly addressed him thus: "Ahem!—I say now—who are you, any way?"

And the man, in his wonder, forgot to take offence, and answered, "Why I, Sir, am the town crier!"

Talk of Yankee cheek indeed!

*On the Stour.*

Then we went on down the lane, past the round marketplace, where women were selling sweets, and under the stone gateway with its time-worn tracery, to the south porch of the Cathedral, where a tricycle was standing. As the pilgrims had to pray before they could approach the sacred tomb, so we, after we had entered the nave, had to wait and listen to morning service. Then we were told that no one could go to the shrine unless led thither by the verger. There was nothing to do but to fall into the ranks of a detachment of tourists on their way to it. With them we were marshalled through the iron gate, separating the choir from the chapels, by a grey-bearded, grey-haired man, who kept his eye sternly upon us as we deposited our sixpences, our modest offerings in place of "silver broch and ryngis."

"Where is the shrine?" we asked, as soon as we were on the other side of the gate.

*Canterbury with Cows.*

"The shrine which it lies but a few steps further on," the verger answered; "and you will come to it in good time."

Then he showed us the "horgan and its pipes, which they lie in the triforium," and the "Norman Chapel of Saint Hanselm, which it is the holdest part of the building," and about all of which he had much to say. But we interrupted him quickly. "Take us to the shrine," we commanded. But just then another tourist, eager for information, began to ask questions not only about the Cathedral, but about the whole city. Before we knew where we were, she had carried us all out to Harbledown, and then, without stopping, whisked us off to Saint Martin's-on-the-Hill. This was too much. We started to find the shrine for ourselves, but our friend the priest ran after us.

"You must wait for the verger," he said. "I hope you don't mind my telling you; but then, you know, you're Americans, and I thought you mightn't understand."

His interest by degrees extended from us to the rest of the party. By some peculiar method of reasoning he had concluded that, because we were Americans, all who were following the verger, except himself, must be so likewise. Every now and then he would dart from our side to ask each one in turn, in a gentle whisper, "You're an American, are you not?" The results were not always satisfactory. I saw one Englishman, with John Bull written in every feature, glare at him in suppressed rage; while a lady, after saying, rather savagely, "Well, is there any harm in being one?" dismissed him abruptly, as if to remind him that not she, but the Cathedral, was the show.

The verger lingered on the broad stairway, "which the pilgrims they mounted it on their knees, as is seen by the two deep grooves in the stone

*Two Pilgrims on Horseback.*

steps." He stood long by the tomb of Prince Hedward, the Black Prince,[33] and when we came to the stone chair used only when archbishops are consecrated, he deliberately stopped, to suggest that some lady might like to sit in it, "though which it won't make her a harchbishop," he added. Then at last he led us to the chapel just beyond, and close to the choir. He waited until we had all followed and formed a semicircle around him, then he pointed to the pavement,—

"Which now," he said, solemnly, "you have come to the shrine of the saintly Thomas."

We had reached our goal. We stood in the holy place for which Monk and Knight, Nun and Wife of Bath, had left husbands and nunnery, castle and monastery, and for which we had braved the jests and jeers of London roughs, and had toiled over the hills and struggled through the sands of Kent. Even the verger seemed to sympathise with our feelings. For a few moments he was silent; presently he continued—

"'Enery the Heighth, when he was in Canterbury, took the bones, which they was laid beneath, out on the green, and had them burned. With them he took the 'oly shrine, which it and bones is here no longer!"

Shrine and Tabard, Chapels and Inns by the way, all have gone with the pilgrims of yester-year.

FINIS.

# An Italian Pilgrimage

BY
JOSEPH & ELIZABETH ROBINS PENNELL.

TO
Charles Godfrey Leland[1]

*who is responsible*
*for our first Work*
*Together*
*&*
*who has been the Great Heart*
*of many a Pilgrimage*
*taken in his*
*Company*
*We*
*Dedicate this*
*Book.*

TO
The Abate of Negro
*of*
*Monte Olive to Maggiore*
*We*
*would say a word of thanks*
*for*
*the Golden Days passed*
*in his House Beautiful*
*and for*
*the great kindnesses*
*shown us in our further*
*journeying.*

## Prefatory Note[2]

These papers were originally published in the *Century*, the *Portfolio*, and *Outing*, the editors kindly allowing us to reprint and recast them. We hope readers who followed us from London to Canterbury may bear with us to the end of the Pilgrimage to Rome, of which our first journey was but the beginning. We warn them that the second stage, from Canterbury to Florence, has been ridden and written, but not yet wrought into a work.

Joseph Pennell,
Elizabeth Robins Pennell.

3, Castle Hill,
Lincoln.

## A Friend's Apology For this Booke

By Charles G. Leland.[3]

Loe! what is this which I'me to sett before ye?
It is, I ween, a very pleasant Story,
How two young Pilgrimes who the World would see,
Did Wheele themselves all over Italy.
One meant to write on't, whence it may be said
That for the Nonce hers was the Wheelwright's trade;
Which is a clever Crafte, for yee have heard
What flits about as a familiar Word
Which in a Workshopp often meets the Eare,
"Bad Wheelwright maketh a good Carpentere!"
If of a bad one such a Saying's true,
Oh what, I pray, may not a good one do?
For by Experience I do declare
'Tis easier to make Books than build a Chaire
*Experto crede*—I have tried them Both,
And sweare a Book is easier—on my Oathe!

He who with her a Pilgriming did go,—
That was her Husband. As this Book doth show,
Rare skill he had when he would Sketches take,
And from those Sketches prittie Pictures make.
She with the Pen could well illuminate,
He with the Pencil Nature illustrate.
Oh, is't not strange that what they did so well
In the Pen way met in the Name PEN-NELL?
By which the Proverb doth approved appeare,
*Nomen est Omen*—as is plaine and cleere.
Which means to say that every Soule doth Bear
A name well suited to his charactere.

Now when this Couple unto Mee did come,
And askt me iff I'de write a little Pome,
That Tale and Picture as they rouled along
Might have some small Accomp'niment of Song,
I set my Pen to Paper with Delighte,
And quickly had my Thoughts in Black and White,
Even as JOHN BUNYAN said he did of yore,
So I, because I'd done the like before.
Since I was the first man of modern time,
Who on the Bicycle e'er wrote a Rime,[4]
How I a Lady in a Vision saw
Upon a Wheel like that of Buddha's Law,
Which kept the Path and went exceeding fast;
Loe! now my Vision is fulfilled at last,
In this brave Writer who with ready Hand
Hath guided well the Wheel ore many a Land,
Showing the World by her adventurous Course,
How one may travel fast as any Horse
Without a Steed, and stop where'er ye will
And have for oats or stable nere a Bill.[5]

As for the Rest—if you but cast your Eye
Upon the Pictures ere the Book ye buy,
And if of Art you are a clever judge,
The Price for it you'll surely not begrudge.
Now, Reader, I have praysed this Booke to Thee,
I trust that Thou wilt scan Itt carefullie;
'Twill set before Thee Portraiture of Townes,
Castles and Towres, antient Villes and Downs,
How rowling Rivers to ye Ocean hast,
Of Road side Inns and many a faire Palast,
Served up, I ween, with so much gentle Mirthe,
Thoulte fairly own thou'st gott thy Money's Worth.
If thou art Cheated Mine shall bee the Sinn,—
Turn o'er the Page, my Lady, and Begin!

———————————

Loe! Vanity Faire! — the Worlde is there,
        Hee and his Wife beside.
Ye may see it afoot, or from the Traine,
        Or if on a Wheel you ride.

*Over the Ponte Vecchio.*

# | An Italian Pilgrimage

## The Start

> "*They are a couple of far countrymen,*
> *and after their mode are going on Pilgrimage.*" [6]

WE STAYED IN FLORENCE THREE DAYS before we started on our pilgrimage to Rome. We needed a short rest. The railway journey straight through from London had been unusually tiresome because of our tricycle. From the first mention of our proposed pilgrimage, kind friends in England had warned us that on the way to Italy the machine would be a burden worse than the Old Man of the Sea. Porters, guards, and custom-house officials would look upon it as lawful prey, and we should pay more to get it to Italy than it had cost in the beginning. It is wonderful how clever one's friends are to discover the disagreeable, and then how eager to point it out!

Our first experience at the station at Holborn Viaduct seemed to confirm their warnings. We paid eight shillings to have the tricycle carried to Dover, porters amiably remarking that it would take a pile of money to get such a machine to Italy. Crossing the Channel, we paid five-and-sixpence more, and the sailors told us condolingly we should have an awful time of it in the custom-house at Calais. This, however, turned out a genuine seaman's yarn. The tricycle was examined carefully, but to be admired, not valued. "That's well made, that!" one guard declared with appreciation, and others playfully urged him to mount it. To make a long story short, our friends proved false prophets.

From Calais to Florence we only paid nine francs freight and thirty-five francs duty at Chiasso.[7] But unfortunately we never knew what might be about to happen. We escaped in one place only to be sure the worst would befal us in the next. It was not until the cause of our anxiety was safe in Florence, that our mental burden was taken away.

But here were more friends who called our pilgrimage a desperate journey, and asked if we had considered what we might meet with in the way we were going. There was the cholera.[8] But we represented that to get to Rome we should not go near the stricken provinces. Then they persisted that our road lay through valleys reeking with malaria until November at least. We should not reach these valleys before November, was our reply. Well then, did we know we must pass through lonely districts where escaped convicts roamed abroad; and in and out of villages where fleas were like unto a plague of Egypt, and good food as scarce as in the wilderness? In a word, ours was a fool's errand. Perhaps it was because so little had come of the earlier prophecies that we gave slight heed to these. They certainly made no difference in our plans. On October 16th, the third morning after our arrival, we rode forth *sans* flea-powder or brandy, *sans* quinine or beef-extract, *sans* everything friends counselled us to take, and hence, according to them, right into the jaws of death.

## In the Val D'Arno

The *padrone*, who helped to strap our portfolio and two bags to the luggage carrier, our coats to the handle bars and the knapsack to J—'s back, and Mr. Mead,[9] the one friend who foretold pleasure, stood at the door of the Hotel Minerva to see us off. The sunlight streamed over the Piazza di Santa Maria Novella, and the beggars on the church-steps and the cabmen, who good-naturedly cried "No carriage for you!" as we wheeled slowly on over to the Via Tornabuoni; past Doni's; by Viessieux's; up the Lung' Arno to the crowded Ponte Vecchio, where for this once at least we were not attacked by the little shopmen; by the Via de' Bardi; then turning into the Borgo San Jacopo; again along the Lung' Arno; and then around with the twisting street-car tracks, through the Porta San Frediano and out on the broad white road which leads to Pisa.[10]

But even before we left Florence we met with our first accident. The luggage carrier swung around from the middle to the side of the backbone.

The one evil consequence, however, was a half-hour's delay. Beyond the gate we stopped at the first blacksmith's. Had either of us known the Italian word for wire, the delay might have been shorter. It was only by elaborate pantomime we could make our meaning clear. Then the blacksmith took the matter in his own hands, unstrapped the bags, and went to work with screw-driver and wire, while the entire neighbourhood, backed by passing pedlars and street car drivers and citizens, pronounced the tricycle "beautiful!" "a new horse!" "a tramway!" When the luggage-carrier was fastened securely, and loaded again, the blacksmith was so proud of his success that he declared "nothing" was his charge. But he was easily persuaded to take something to drink the *Signore's* health. After this there were no further stops.

Our road for some distance went over streets laid with the great stones of the old Tuscan pavement,[11]—and for tricyclers these streets are not very bad going—between tall grey houses, with shrines built in them, and those high walls which radiate from Florence in every direction, and keep one from seeing the gardens and green places within. Women, plaiting straw, great yellow bunches of which hung at their waists, and children greeted us with shouts. Shirtless bakers their hands white with flour, and barbers holding their razors, men with faces half shaved and still lathered, and others with wine-glasses to their lips, rushed to look at this new folly of the foreigner, for ours was the first tandem tricycle ever seen in Italy. At Signa, on the steep up-grade just outside the town, we had a lively spurt with a dummy engine, the engineer apparently trying to run us down as we were about to cross the track. After this we rode between olives and vineyards where there were fewer people. There was not a cloud in the sky, so blue overhead and so white above the far hill-tops on the horizon. The wind in the trees rustled gently in friendliness. Solemn, white-faced, broad-horned oxen stared at us sympathetically over the hedges. One young peasant even stopped his cart to say how beautiful he thought it must be to travel in Italy after our fashion. All day we passed grey olive-gardens and green terraced hill-sides, narrow Tuscan-walled streams, dry at this season and long rows of slim, straight poplars,—white trees, a woman told us was their name. Every here and there was a shrine with lamp burning before the Madonna, or a wayside cross bearing spear and scourge and crown of thorns. Now we rode by the fair river of Arno, where reeds grew tall and close by the water's edge, and where the grey-green mountains rising almost from its banks were barren of all trees save dark stone-pines and towering cypresses, like so many mountains in Raphael's or Perugino's pictures.[12] Now

*In the Sunlight.*

we came to where the plain broadened and the mountains were blue and distant. Mulberries, the peasants had stripped of their leaves before their time, but not bare because of the vines festooned about them, broke with their even ranks the monotony of grey and brown ploughed fields. Here on a hill was a white villa or monastery, with long lofty avenue of cypresses; there, the stanch unshaken walls and gates of castle or fortress, which, however, had long since disappeared. It is true all these things are to be seen hastily from the windows of the railroad train. But it is only by following the windings and long straight stretches of the road as we did, stopping now and then or riding slowly, that its great loveliness can be felt and known, as it must have been by the men of old, who understood so well how to make beautiful their longest journeys. Later in the afternoon, with a turn of the road, we came suddenly in view of Capraia, high up above, and far to the other side of the river; so far, indeed, that all detail was lost, and we could only see the mass of its houses and towers and *campanile*,[13] washed into the whitish-blue sky. And all the time we were working just hard enough to feel that joy of mere living which comes with healthy out-of-door exercise, and, I think, with nothing else.

Sometimes we rode, seeing no one and hearing no other sound than the low cries of a cricket in the hedge or the loud calls of an unseen ploughman in a neighbouring field. Then an old woman went by, complimenting us on going

*A Perugino Landscape.*

so fast without a horse; and then a baker's boy in white shirt and bare legs, carrying a lamb on his shoulders. But then, again, we met wagon after wagon, piled with boxes and baskets, poultry and vegetables, and sleeping men and women, and with lanterns swinging between the wheels;—for the next day would be Friday and market-day, and peasants were already on their way to Florence. There were pedlars, too, walking from village to village, selling straw fans and gorgeous handkerchiefs. Would not the Signora have a handkerchief? one asked, showing me the gayest of his stock. For answer I pointed to the bags on the luggage-carrier and the knapsack on J—'s back. Of course, he said. We already had enough to carry. Would the *Signora* forgive him for troubling her? And with a polite bow he went on his way.

We came to several villages and towns,—some small, where pots and bowls, fresh from the potter's wheel, were set out to dry; others large, like Lastra, with heavy walls and gates, and old archways, and steps leading up to crooked, steep streets, so narrow that the sun never shines into them; or like Montelupo, where for a while we sat on the bridge without the farther gate, looking at the houses which climb up the hill-side to the cypress-encircled monastery at the top. Women were washing in the stream below, and under the poplars on the bank a priest in black robes and broad-brimmed hat walked with a young lady. But whenever we stopped, children from far and near

*Street in Lastra.*

collected around us. There were little old-fashioned girls, with handkerchiefs tied over their heads in womanly fashion, who kept on plaiting straw, and small boys nursing big babies, their hands and mouths full of bread and grapes. If, however, in their youthful curiosity they pressed upon us too closely, polite men and women, who had also come to look, drove them back with terrible cries of *Via, ragazzi!* (go away, children!), before which they retreated with the same speed with which they had advanced.

Just beyond Montelupo, when a tedious up-grade brought us to a broad plateau, a cart suddenly came out a little way in front of us from a side road. A man was driving, and on the seat behind, and facing us, were two nuns who wore wide straw hats, which flapped slowly up and down with the motion of the cart. When they saw us, the younger of the two covered her face with her hands as if she thought us a device of the devil. But the other, who looked the Lady Abbess, met the danger bravely and sternly examined us. This close scrutiny reassured her. When we drew nearer she wished us good evening, and then her companion turned and looked. We told them we were pilgrims bound for Rome. At this they took courage, and the spokeswoman begged for the babies they cared for in Florence. We gave her a few sous. She counted them quite greedily, and then—but not till then—benevolently blessed us. They were going at jog-trot pace, so that we soon left them behind. "*Buono viaggio,*"[14] the Abbess cried, and the silent sister smiled, showing all her pretty white teeth, for we now represented a temptation overcome. [15]

*On the Arno, near Empoli.*

## At Empoli

We put up that night at Empoli. The Albergo Maggiore was fair enough, and, like all large Italian inns had a clean, spacious stable in which to shelter the tricycle. The only drawback to our comfort was the misery at dinner of the black-eyed, blue-shirted waiter at our refusal to eat a dish of birds we had not ordered. He was very eager to dispose of them. He served them with every course, setting them on the table with a triumphant cry of *Ecco!* as if he had prepared a delicious surprise. It was not until he brought our coffee that he despaired. Then he retired mournfully to the kitchen, where his loud talk with the *padrona* made us fear their wrath would fall upon us or the tricycle. But later they gave us candles, and said good-night with such gracious smiles that we slept the sleep which knows neither care nor fear.

The next morning their temper was as unclouded as the sky. They both watched the loading of the tricycle with smiling interest. He had seen many a *velocipede* with two wheels, the waiter said, but never one with three. And that a *Signora* should ride, the *padrona* added, ah! that indeed was strange! Then she grew confidential. Only occasionally I caught her meaning, for my knowledge of Italian was small. She had had seven children, she said, and all were dead but one. And I, had I any? And where had I bought my dress? She liked it so much, and she took it in her hand and felt it. Should we stay long in Italy? and some time we would come back to Empoli? Her son, a little fellow, was there too. He had been hanging about the machine when we came down to breakfast and ever since. He stood speechless while J— was by, but when the latter went away for a few minutes—less shy with me I suppose because he knew I could not understand him as well—he asked, what might such a *velocipede* cost? as much perhaps as a hundred francs? But J— coming back he was silent as before. They all followed us out to the street, the *padrona* shaking hands with us both, and the boy standing by the tricycle to the very last.

## The Road to Fair and Soft Siena

It was good to be in the open country again, warming ourselves in the hot sunshine. The second morning of our ride was better than the first. We knew beforehand how beautiful the day would be, and how white and smooth was the road that lay before us. The white oxen behind the ploughs, and the mules in their gay trappings and shining harness, seemed like old acquaintances. The pleasant good morning given us by every peasant we met made us forget we were strangers in the land. A little way from Empoli we crossed the Ponte d'Elsa, and then, after a sharp turn to the right, we were on the road to "fair and soft Siena." It led on through vineyards and wide fields lying open to the sun, by sloping hill-sides and narrow, winding rivers, by villas and gardens where roses were blooming. In places they hung over the wall into the road. We asked a little boy to give us one. For the *Signora*, J— added. But the child shook his head. How could he? The roses were not his, he said. Once we passed a wayside cross on which loving hands had laid a bunch of the fresh blossoms. Sometimes we heard from the far-away mountains the loud blasting of rocks and then the soft bells of a monastery; sometimes the cracking of the whip of a peasant behind us, driving an unwilling donkey. Then we would pass from the stillness of the country into the noise and clamour of small villages, to hear the wondering cries of the women to which we were already growing accustomed, the piercing yells of babies, who, well secured in basket go-carts, could not get to us quickly enough, and the sing-song repetition of older children saying their lessons in school, and whom we could see at their work through the low windows. About noon we rode into Certaldo, Boccaccio's town.[16] I know nothing that interferes so seriously with hero-worship as hunger. I confess that if some one had said, "You can go either to see Boccaccio's house, or to lunch at a *trattoria*,[17] but both these things you cannot do," our answer would have been an immediate order for lunch. We went at once to a trattoria on the piazza where Boccaccio's statue stands. I doubt if that great man himself ever

*At the Foot of the Cross.*

gathered such numbers about him as we did. Excited citizens, when the tricycle
was put away, stood on the threshold and stared at us until the door was shut
upon them. Then they pressed their faces against the windows and peered
over piles of red and yellow pears, and every now and then one, bolder than the
rest, stealthily thrust his head in and then scampered off before he could be
captured. This gave a spice of novelty and excitement to our midday meal.

We ordered a very simple lunch; soup, bread and cheese, coffee and
vermouth. But the *padrona* had to send out for everything. Her sister, a young
girl as fair as an English-woman, was her messenger. We were scarcely seated
before she came back with coffee and a large bottle which she set before us.
This of course was the vermouth, and we half filled our glasses and at once
drank a little. The two women stared with a surprise we could not understand.
The fair girl now disappeared on a second foraging expedition and stayed away
until we had finished our soup. "*Ecco, vermouth!*" she said on her return putting

*San Gimignano delle belle Torre.*

another bottle in front of us. Then we knew the reason of their wonder. We had swallowed, like so much water, the not over strong cognac intended only to flavour our coffee. Presently the *padrona* entered into conversation with us. We were English, she supposed. No, Americans, we told her. At this there was great rejoicing. They had a brother in America. He lived in a large town called Buenos Ayres, where he kept a *trattoria*. Like theirs it was the *Trattoria Boccaccio*. They were glad to see any one from the same country, whether from North or South. Was it not all America? The *padrona* went up stairs to bring down his picture that we might see it. Her sister pointed to the purple woollen jersey she wore and said with pride her brother had sent it to her. It too was American. They even called in their old mother that she might see her son's fellow-countrymen.

We spent an hour wandering through the old town on top of the hill in which Boccaccio really lived. The sun was shining right down into the streets in which the gay kerchiefs of the women, the bunches of straw at their waists, and their cornstalk distaffs made bright bit of colour. Though we left the tricycle at the *trattoria*, our coming made a stir in the upper town. Our clothes were not like unto those of the natives, and J—'s knee-breeches and long black stockings made them wonder what manner of priest he might be. As we stood looking at the *loggia*[18] and tower and arched doorway of Boccaccio's house, the custodian with a heavy bunch of keys came to take us through it. But we declined his services. We cared more for the old streets and walls and palaces,

*San Gimignano close up.*

which, though their greatness has gone, have not been changed since medi-aeval times, than for an interior, however fine, whose mediaevalism dates from to-day. The old man turned away rather sulkily. J— seeing there had been some mistake, explained that we had not sent for him. Then his face cleared. The women had said we wanted him, else he would never have disturbed us, and he took off his hat and this time went away with a friendly *a rivederle*.[19]

The Palazzo Communale, at the highest point of the town, is still covered with the arms and insignia of other years, of the Medici and Piccolomini, of the Orsini and Baglioni.[20] Its vaulted doorway is still decorated with frescoes of the Madonna, and saints and angels. But everywhere the plaster is falling away, and in the courtyard grass grows between the bricks of the pavement, and instead of pages and men-at-arms we there saw only a little brown-faced ragged child climbing cat like over the roofs, and a woman scolding him from below. We left the town by the city gate, through which we saw the near hills grey, bare, and furrowed, the long lines of cypresses, the stretches of grey olives, the valley below with its vineyards, and the far mountains, purple and shadowy, the highest topped with many-towered San Gimignano.

It is better not to be jocund with the fruitful grape in the middle of the day when one is tricycling. The cognac we had taken at lunch, weak as it was, and the vermouth made us sleepy and our feet heavy. I sympathised with the men who lay in sound slumbers in every cart we met. But their drowsiness forced us into wakefulness. Of the ride from Certaldo to Poggibonsi, I remember best the loud inarticulate cries of J— and his calls of *"Eccomi!"*[21] as if he were lord of the land, to sleeping drivers. The Italian cry of the roads, rising to a high note and then suddenly falling and ending in a low prolonged one, which is indispensable to travellers, is not easy to learn. J—'s proficiency in it, however, when he limited himself to howling, made him pass for a native. But often donkeys darted into ditches and oxen plunged across the road before the peasants behind them awoke. Like Sancho Panza they had a talent for sleeping.

Once, after we had climbed a short but steep hill and had passed by several wagons in rapid succession, we stopped in the shade to take rest. It was a pleasant place. We looked over the broad valley, where the vines were festooned, not as Virgil saw them,[22] from elm to elm, but from mulberry to mulberry, and up to San Gimignano, beginning to take more definite shape on its mountain-top. A peasant in peaked hat and blue shirt, with trousers rolled up high above his bare knees, crossed the road and silently examined the tricycle. "You have a good horse," he then said; "it eats nothing." We asked him if they were at work in his vineyard. No, he answered; but would we like to look in the wine-press opposite? And then he took us through the dark windowless building, where on one side the grape-juice was fermenting in large butts, and on the other fresh grapes had been laid on sets of shelves to dry. He picked out two of the finest bunches and gave them to me. When I offered to pay him he refused. The Signora must accept them, he said.

As the road was now a dead level and lumpy into the bargain we were glad when Poggibonsi was in sight. We drew up on a bridge, where a man was standing, to ask him if he knew of a good inn. He recommended the Albergo dell' Aquila. "It is good," he went on, "and not too dear. This is not a town where they take one by the neck," and he clutched his own throat. So to the Albergo dell' Aquila we went. We had only to ride through the wide avenue of shady trees, past a row of houses, out of one of which a brown-robed monk came, to rush back at sight of us, past a washing-place surrounded by busy chattering women, and we were at the door of the inn.

## At Poggibonsi

The inn was even more comfortable than the Albergo Maggiore in Empoli. We dined in a room from whose walls King Humbert[23] and his queen smiled upon us, while opposite were two sensational and suggestive brigands in lonely mountain passes.

The *padrona* came up with the salad, and she and the waiter in a cheerful duet catechised us after the friendly Italian fashion, and then told us about the visit to their house of the American consul from Florence, of the hard times the cholera had brought with it for all Italy, of the bad roads to San Gimignano and the steep ones to Siena, along which peasants never travelled without bearing in mind the old saying: "*All' ingiù tutti i santi ajutano; ma all' insú ci vuol Gesù.*" ("Going down hill, call upon the saints; but going up one needs Jesus.") Before long J— joined in the talk, and the duet became a trio. Never had I been so impressed with his fluent Italian. Even the *padrona* was not readier with her words than he with his. When I spoke to him about it afterwards, he said he supposed it was wonderful; he had not understood half of it himself.

After dinner and in the twilight we walked through the lively crowded streets and into the church, where service was just over. A priest in white surplice left the altar, and another began to put the lights out when we entered. But in the unlit nave many of the faithful still knelt in prayer. The town grew quieter as night came on, but just as we were going to sleep some men went along the street below our window singing. One in a loud clear tenor sang the tune; the others the accompaniment like a part song, and the effect was that of a great guitar. Their song was a fitting good-night to a day to whose beauty there had been not a cloud.

## In the Mountains

Though we left Poggibonsi in the beginning of the morning, a large crowd waited for us at the door of the inn. The *padrona* said farewell with many good wishes; men and women we had never seen before called out pleasantly *a rivederle*, two *carabinieri*[24] watched us from the other side of the piazza, the railroad officials at the station cried, *Partenza! Partenza!*[25] and then we were off and out of the town.

It would be *su, su, su*[26] all the way, they told us at the inn, but for several miles we went fast enough, so that I felt sure the peasants we passed were still only calling on the saints. The ascent at first was very gradual, while the road was excellent. There were down as well as up grades, and for every steep climb we had a short coast. Now we came out on villas which but a little before had been above us, and now we reached the very summit of hills from which we looked forth upon mountain rising beyond mountain—some treeless and ashen grey, others thickly wooded and glowing with golden greens and russets, and still others white and mist-like, and seeming to melt into the soft white clouds resting on their highest peaks. All along, the hedges were covered with clusters of red rose-berries and the orange berries of the pyracanthus. The grass by the roadside was gay with brilliant crimson pinks, yellow snap-dragons, and dandelions, and violet daisies. Once we came to a vineyard where the ripe fruit still hung in purple clusters from the vines, and where men and women, some on foot and others on ladders, were gathering and filling with them large buckets and baskets. At the far end of the field white oxen, their great heads decorated with red ribbons, stood in waiting. Boys with buckets slung on long poles were coming and going between the vines. In all the other vineyards we had passed the vintage had been over, so we waited to watch the peasants, as, laughing and singing, they worked away. But when they saw us, they too stopped and looked, and one man came down from his ladder and to the hedge to offer us a bunch of grapes.

The only town through which we rode was Staggia, where workmen were busy restoring the old tower and making it a greater ruin than it had ever been before. One town gate has gone, but from the battlements of the other grass and weeds still wave with the wind, while houses have been built into the broken walls. It is a degenerate little town, and its degeneracy, paradoxical as it may sound, is the result of its activity. For its inhabitants have not rested content like those of Lastra with the medievalism that surrounds them. They have striven to make what is old new by painting their church and many of their houses in that scene-painting style which today seems to represent the art of the people in Italy. Often during our journey we saw specimens of this vile fashion—houses with sham windows and shutters, churches with make-believe curtains and cords—but nowhere was it so prominent as in Staggia.

Beyond Monteriggione, whose towers alone showed above its high walls, the road began to wind upward on the mountain-side. It was such a long, steady pull that although the surface was perfect we gave up riding and walked. Our machine was heavily loaded and not too easy to work over prolonged up-grades. Besides, we were not time nor record makers nor perambulating advertisements, and we had the day before us. We were now closed in with woods; on either side were chestnuts and dwarf oaks and bushes, their leaves all "yellow and black and pale and hectic red."[27] And occasional openings showed near mountain-tops covered with downy grey grass and a low growth like heather, and here and there were groups of dark pines. For an hour at least we were alone with the sounds and silence of the mountains. The wandering wind whispered in the wood, and black swine rooted in the fallen leaves, but of human life there was no sign. Then there came from afar a regular tap-tap, low at first, but growing louder and louder, until, as we drew closer to it, we knew it to be the steady hammering of stone-breakers. There were two men at work in this lonely pass, and as we stood talking to them two more came from under the chestnuts. These had guns on their shoulders, and wore high boots and the high-crowned conventional brigand hat. Ever since we left Florence we had seen at intervals in the fields and woods a notice with the words, "*E vietata la bandita*,"[28] which we had interpreted as a warning against the bandits or convicts for whom our Florentine friends had prepared us. And now we seemed to have come face to face with two of these brigands. But it turned out there was little of the bandit about them save their appearance. Their guns were for birds, and later on we learned that the alarming signs were merely to forbid the trespassing of these very gentlemen.

A mile or two further on the road began to go down again. We were both glad to be on the machine after our walk. We could see to the bottom of the hill, and there was no one in sight. J— let go the brake. None but cyclers know the delight of a five minutes' coast after hours of up-hill toiling. They, however, will sympathise with our pleasure in the mountains near Siena. But when it was at its fullest, and the machine was going at the rate of about twenty miles an hour, and neither brake nor back-pedalling could bring it to a sudden halt, a man, or the foul fiend himself, drove a flock of sheep out from the woods a few feet in front of us. When we reached them only the first had crossed the road. Of course, all the rest had to follow. They tried to go on right through the wheels, but only succeeded in getting under them, setting the machine pitching like a ship in a heavy sea. But I held on fast, J— stood on the pedals and screwed the brake down,[29] the little wheel scattered the sheep like the cow-catcher of an engine, and we brought up in the gutter. Before we stopped J— began a moral lecture to the shepherd, and was showing him how if the machine had gone over, the consequences would have been worse for us than for his flock. The lecture ended rather immorally with *Accidente voi*, and *Imbecile*, the deadliest of all Italian maledictions, punishable in places by

*A Slight Obstruction.*

imprisonment. The shepherd looked as if he was ready to curse us in return, but before he had time to form an expression suitable to the occasion, we were out of hearing, though we first made sure that no sheep were hurt. We were none the worse for the accident, and the tricycle was uninjured, save for a deep dent in the dress guard.[30]

The rest of our way was divided between walking and riding. The woods with their solitude and wildness—but not the good road—came to an end. Once beyond them we wheeled out by fields where men and women were at work, their oxen whiter than any we had yet seen by contrast with the rich red of the upturned earth. In olive-gardens peasants were eating their mid-day meal; men with white aprons, women with enormous Sienese hats, and dogs and oxen were all resting sociably together. By the roadside others were making rope, the men twisting and for ever walking backwards, a small boy always turning at the wheel. Scattered on the hill-tops and by the road were large red-brick farm-houses, instead of the white ones we had seen near Florence. At one where there was a well on the other side of the wall, we asked for a glass of water. A man brought it to the gate, where he was joined by three or four others. They stared inquiringly at the tricycle, at the bags and at us while J— squeezed lemon juice into the water. Then one opened his mouth very wide and pointed to his teeth: "The little sir," he asked, "is he a dentist?" And so we were taken for an advertisement after all. Only the evening before we had seen at Poggibonsi by many posters that a travelling dentist was to pass that way.

*Noontide.*

It was noon when we first saw Siena, and we were then at the very walls. In the old days it was always said, "More than her gates, Siena opens her heart to you!" But the heart of him who sat in office by the city gate was shut against us. When we rode past him he bade us descend. To our "*Perche*?"[31] he said it was the law. Oh the vanity of these Sienese! Through the streets of Florence and over the crowded Ponte Vecchio we had ridden undisturbed, but in this mountain town, which boasts of but two hacks, and where donkeys and oxen are the only beasts to be frightened, we were forced to get down. The dignity of the law-makers of the city must be respected! So we two weary pilgrims had to walk along the narrow streets, between the tall palaces, while tanners in red caps, and women in flowered, white-ribboned hats, and priests and soldiers stared, and one man, with a long push-cart, kept close to us like an evil genius in a dream. He was now on one side and now on the other, examining the wheels, asking endless questions, and always getting in the way. At all the street corners he hurried on before, and with loud shouts called the people to come and see. Then he was at our heels again, shrieking his loud, shrill trade cry into our very ears. J— as a rule is not ill-tempered; but there is a limit to all things. The stupid sheep, the watchful guard, and now this plague of a flower-pedlar brought his patience to an end, and on our way through the town he said much in good plain English which it was well the citizens could not understand.

## Fair and Soft Siena

Even pilgrims of old, on their way to Rome, sometimes tarried in castle or village. We could not pass through Siena, discourteous though her first welcome had been, as we had through smaller and less fair towns. So for a day or two we put away our tricycle, and the "cockle-shells and sandal shoon"[32] of our pilgrimage. We went to a *pension*, one at which J— had stayed before, and which he liked.[33] I admit it was better in many ways than the inns in which we had hitherto slept and eaten. There was carpet on the floor of our room, and in it easy-chairs and a lounge. There were elaborate breakfasts at one and still more elaborate dinners at six, and there was always a great plenty, as the Englishwoman who sat next to me, and who, I fear, had not always fared so well, said, when she urged me to eat and drink more of the fruit and wine set before me. "You can have all you want in this house," she finished with a sigh, as if her crown of sorrow was in remembering *unhappier* things. But we both thought regretfully of the dining-rooms with the bad prints on the walls, and the more modest dinners of our own ordering. I think, too, we had found more pleasure in the half-understood talk of *padroni* and waiters than we did now in the elegant and learned conversation of our fellow-boarders, for they were all, it seemed, persons of learning and refinement. There was the retired English major-general who sat opposite, and who had written a book, as he very soon let us know. He recognised us as Americans before we opened our mouths to speak, which fact he also let us know by his reminiscences addressed not to us, but to our neighbours. He had travelled in Spain with Mr. Fillmore, the ex-President, "the most courteous of gentlemen."[34] He said he well knew Mr. Marion Crawford,[35] the talented novelist, and his uncle, "dear old Sam Ward."[36] He had counted among his best friends Ba-yard Taylor,[37] "as you remember I have said in my book." This same book which made the major so communicative appeared to have crushed the spirit out of his wife, who sat silent during dinner. Then there was the elderly English lady travelling abroad with her daughter, who "has just taken up architecture," she informed us; "she has always painted heads till now, but she is so fascinated by her architectural work. Then I, you know, am so fond of water colours." And there was the Swedish lady, who could talk all languages, speaking to us in something supposed to be English, and who was as eager in her pursuit of food for her body as for her mind. I count the way in which she greedily swallowed the *vino santo* in her glass, when our host passed around the table the second time with his precious bottle, one of the wonders of our visit to Siena. It was pathetic too to see her disappointment when he turned away, just before he reached her, his bottle empty. And there were still others who knew much about pictures and palaces, statues and studios, and no doubt we might greatly have profited thereby; but we liked it better up stairs, where we were alone and there was less culture. Our window over-looked a high terrace in which marigolds and many-coloured chrysanthemums were blooming, the gardens of the Piccolomini Palace full of broad-leaved fig-trees and pale olives, and the wide waste of mountain and moorland stretching from the red city walls to the high, snow-capped Apennines on the horizon. All the morning the sun shone in our windows, and every hour and even oftener we heard the church bells, and the loud, clear bugle-calls from the barracks, once a monastery, whose mass of red and grey walls rose from the near olives. They say it snows in Siena in the winter-time, and that it is cold and bleak and dreary, but I shall always think of it as a place of flowers and sunshine and sweet sounds.

But best of all were the hours when we wandered through the town, up and down dark alley-ways and flights of steps, under brick arches, along precipitate, narrow streets, where we had to press close to the houses, or retreat into an open door, to let the wide-horned oxen pass by with their load; now coming out at the very foot of La Mangia, on the broad, sunny *piazza*; now by the tanneries, where little streams of brown water trickled down towards the washing-place at the foot of the hill, and where the walls were hung with dripping brown skins, probably just as they were when the little Catherine, her visions already beginning, and Stefano walked by them and towards home in the fading evening light, from a visit to the older and married sister Bonaventura.[38] One hour we were with the past in the shadowy aisles of the *Duomo*, where Moses and Hermes Trismegistus,[39] Solomon and Socrates, Sibyls and Angels looked up at us from the pavement, and rows of popes kept watch from above the tall black and white pillars, while in the choir beyond priests chanted their solemn psalms. Next we were with the present in the gay Lizza, under the acacias and yellow chestnuts, by flower-beds full of roses and scarlet sage, and walls now covered with brilliant Virginia creepers; and out on the fort above to see a golden sky, and the sun disappearing behind banks of purple, golden-edged, and red clouds, and pale, misty hills; to look back across the gulf to the red town climbing up from low olive gardens towards the *Duomo* on its hill-top and tall La Mangia springing aloft from its own little hollow beyond. From every side came the voices of many people; of soldiers in the barracks, of women and children under the trees, of ball players in the old court below, and of applauding lookers-on lounging on the marble benches.

The tall unfinished arch of the *Duomo* that rises above houses and churches, and indeed above everything but the lofty La Mangia and the *Campanile*, tells the story of greatness and power and wealth suddenly checked. But the deadly plague,[40] which carried off so many citizens that not even enough were left to make their city beautiful as they meant she should be, could not take away the beauty that was already hers nor kill the joyousness of her people.

There are no Spendthrift Clubs[41] in Siena now, nor any gay Lanos, like him Dante met in the *Inferno*.[42] But there are still laughter and song-loving Sienese, who, in their own simple fashion, go through life gathering rose-buds while they may. It seemed to us a very pretty fashion when we saw them holiday making on Sunday afternoon, peasants, priests, officers, townspeople, all out in their Sunday best, and when on the Via Cavour, near the *loggia*, we met two wandering minstrels singing love-songs through the town. One played on a mandoline which hung from his neck by a wide red ribbon, and as he played he sang. His voice was loud and strong and very sweet, and like another Orpheus[43] he drew after him all who heard his music. His companion sold copies of the song, printed on pink paper, gay as the words. He went, bowing and smiling, in and out of the crowd; from the women, whose broad hats waved as they kept time to the singing, to the men who had stuck feathers in their soft felts, worn jauntily on one side, from demure little girls holding their nurses' hands to swaggering soldiers. Then when the first singer rested, he, in his turn, sang a verse. There was with them a small boy who every now and then broke in in a high treble, so that there was no pause in the singing.

Wherever we went that afternoon, whether by the *Duomo* or out by the Porta Romana, on the Lizza or near San Domenico, we saw large written posters, announcing that at six in the evening there would be, at No. 17, Via Ricasoli, a great marionette performance of the *Ponte dei Sospiri*.[44] Apparently this was to be the event of the day, and to it we determined to go. When a little before the appointed hour we came to the Via Ricasoli, we half expected to see a theatre ablaze with light. What we did find, after much difficulty, was a low doorway on the ground floor of a many-storied palace, and before it a woman by a table, lighting a very small lamp, to the evident satisfaction of half a dozen youngsters. Over the open doorway was a chintz curtain. Behind it, darkness. This was not encouraging. But presently a woman with a child came to buy

*By the River.*

tickets. One of the group of youthful admirers was then sent up, and a second down, the street, and after they had come back with mysterious bundles, another lamp was produced, lit, and carried inside, and the first two of the audience followed. It was now within five minutes of six, so we also bought our tickets, three *soldi*, or cents, for each, and the curtain was drawn for us. A low, crypt-like room with vaulted ceiling; at one end two screens covered with white sheets; between them a stage somewhat larger than that of a street Punch,[45] with a curtain representing a characteristic Sienese brick wall inclosing a fountain; several rows of rough wooden benches, and one of chairs—this was what we saw by the dim light of one lamp. We sat on the last bench. The audience probably would be more entertaining than the play. But the humble shall be exalted. The woman on the front row bade us come up higher. The small boy, who acted as usher told us we might have two of the chairs for two *soldi* more. The ticket-seller even came in, and in soft, pleading tones said that we might have any places we wanted; why then should we choose the worst? But we refused the exaltation.

The audience now began to arrive in good earnest. Five ragged boys of the *gamin*[46] species, one of a neater order with his little sister by the hand, two soldiers, a lady with a blue feather in her bonnet and her child and nurse, two young girls, and the benches were almost filled. Our friend the ticket-seller became very active as business grew brisk. She was always running in and out, now giving this one a seat, now rearranging the reserved chairs, and now keeping the younger members of the audience in order. Her manner was gentle and insinuating. *Ragazzini*,[47] she called the unruly boys who stood up on the benches and whistled and sang, so that I wondered what diminutive she gave the swells on the front row. This was amusing enough, but our dinner hour was half-past six. J— looked at his watch. It was a quarter past. The ever-watchful keeper of the show saw him. "Ah! the *Signore* must not be impatient. *Ecco!* the music was about to begin." Begin it did indeed, to be continued with a persistency which made us fear it would never end. The musicians were two. A young man in a velveteen coat and long yellow necktie played the clarionet and another the cornet. They only knew one tune—a waltz, I think it was meant to be—but that they gave without stint, playing it over and over again, even while the ticket-seller made them move from their chairs, to a long high box by the wall; and when a third arrived with a trombone they let him join in when and as it best pleased him. When we had heard at least the twenty-fifth repetition of the waltz; had looked at the scuffling of the *ragazzini* until even that pleasure palled; had seen the soldiers smoke *cigaro Cavour*[48] after *cigaro Cavour* so that the air grew heavy; and had watched the gradual growth of the audience until every place was filled, our patience was exhausted. Behold! we said to the woman with the gentle voice, it was now seven. The play was announced for six. Was this right? In a house not far off every one was eating, and two covers were laid for us. But here we were in this dark room in our hunger, waiting for marionettes whose wires for aught we knew were broken! She became penitent. The *Signorini* must forgive her. The wires were not broken, but he who pulled them had not come. There was yet time. Would we not go and dine and then come back? She would admit us on our return.

And so we went and had our dinner, well seasoned with polite conversation. The ticket agent was true to her word. When we re-appeared at her door, the curtain was pulled at once. In the meantime the musicians had been suppressed, not only out of hearing but out of sight. The room was so crowded that many who had arrived during our absence were standing. Indeed, by this time, there must have been at least five francs in the house. All were watching with entranced eyes the movements of four or five puppets. The scene represented an interior which, I suppose, was that of the prison on one side of the Bridge of Sighs. That it was intended for a cell also seemed evident, because the one portable piece of furniture on the stage was a low flat couch of a shape which, as every one who has been to the theatre, but never to prison, knows, is peculiar to the latter. It was impossible to lose sight of it, as the *dramatis personae* made their exits and entrances over it. It was rather funny to see the villain of the piece after an outbreak of passion, or an elegant long-haired page in crimson clad, after a gentlemanly speech, suddenly vault over it. We could not discover what the play was about. Besides the two above-mentioned characters, there was a puppet with a large red face and green coat and trousers who gave moral tone to the dialogue, and another with heavy black beard and turban-like headdress, and much velvet and lace, whom we took to be a person of rank. As they came in and out by turn, it was impossible to decide which was the prisoner. With the exception of the jumps over the couch, there was little action in the performance. Its only two noticeable features were: first, the fact that villain, page, moralist, and magnate spoke in exactly the same voice and with the same expression; and, secondly, that they had an irrepressible tendency to stand in the air rather than on the floor, as if they had borrowed Mr. Stockton's negative gravity machine.[49] The applause and laughter and rapt attention of the audience proved the play to be much to their liking. But for us inappreciative foreigners a little of it went a great way. As nothing but talk came of all the villainy and moralising and grandeur and prettiness—which may have been a clever bit of realism of which the English drama is not yet capable—and as there was no apparent reason why the dialogue should ever come to an end, we went away after the next act. The ticket-seller was surprised at our sudden change from eagerness to indifference, but not offended. She thanked us for our patronage, and wished us a *felice notte*.[50]

With the darkness the gaiety of the town had increased. In the large theatre a play was being performed by a company of amateurs. Having had tickets given us, we looked in for a few minutes, but found it as wordy as that of the puppets. In a neighbouring piazza the proprietor of a large van, much like those to be seen in country fairs at home, was exhibiting a man, arrayed in a suit of rubber with a large brass helmet-like arrangement on his head, who, it seemed, could live at the bottom of the sea, along with Neptune and the

Naiads, as comfortably as on dry shore. *Ecco!* There was the tank within where this marvel could be seen—a human being living under the water, and none the worse for it! Admission was four *soldi*, but *per militari e ragazzi*—for military and children—it was but two! So it seems that the soldiers, who abroad are to strike terror into the enemy, at home are ranked with the young of the land, since like them their name is legion! There were about a dozen in the crowd, and, all unconscious of the sarcasm, they hurried up the steps and into the show, while an old man ground out of a hand-organ the appropriate tune of *O que faime les militaires.*[51]

But dramas and shows were not the only Sunday evening amusements. The *caffe* were crowded. Judging from the glimpses we had into little black cavern-like wine-shops, another Saint Bernardino[52] is needed to set makers of gaming tools in Siena to the manufacture of holier articles. And more than once, as we walked homewards in the starlight, we heard the voices of three minstrels singing of human passion in the streets where Catherine so often preached the rapture of divine love. If swans were now seen in visions by fond Sienese matrons, they would wing their way earthward, and not heavenward as in the days when Blessed Bernardo's mother dreamed dreams.

## An Italian By-Road

We left Siena the morning after the Marionette Exhibition. The Major when he heard at breakfast that we were going, asked us point blank several questions about Boston publishers, his book probably being still uppermost in his thoughts. Later he sent his card to our room to know at what hour we started. He wished to see us off. The young lady of architectural proclivities shook hands and bade us good-bye, saying she had often ridden a sociable with her cousin in England.[53]

After all there was not much for the Major to see. We could not ride through the streets, and so could not mount the machine for his benefit. But he was interested in watching us strap the bags to the luggage carrier, and pleased because of this opportunity to entertain us with more American reminiscences. I am afraid his amusement in Siena was small. In return for the little we gave him he asked us to come and see him in Rome, where he would spend the winter, and added that if we expected to pass through Cortona he would like to write a card of introduction for us to a friend of his there, an Italian who had married an English lady. Cortona was a rough place, and we might be glad to have it. He had forgotten his friend's name, but he would run up stairs and his wife could tell him. In a minute he returned with the written card. We have had many letters of introduction, but never one as singular as the Major-general's. As he knew our name even less well than that of his Cortona friend's, he introduced us as an "American lady and gentleman riding a *bicycle!*" Only fancy! as the English say. Our parting with him was friendly. Then he stood with Luigi and Zara until we disappeared round the corner of the street.

What a ride we had from Siena to Buonconvento! This time the road was all *giù, giù, giù*.[54] It was one long coast almost all the way, and we made the most of it. We flew by milestone after milestone. Once we timed ourselves: we made a mile in four minutes. The country through which we rode was sad and desolate. On each side were low, rolling hills, bare as the English moors, and of every shade of grey and brown and purple. Here rose a hill steeper than the others, with a black cross on its summit; and here, one crowned with a group of four grim cypresses. Down the hillsides were deep ruts and gullies, with only an occasional patch of green, where women were watching sheep and swine. Once we came to three or four houses gathered round a small church, but they were as desolate as the land. We heard voices in the distance, but there was no one in sight. When on a short stretch of level road we stopped to look at this strange grey land, the greyer because dark clouds covered the sky, we saw that above the barrenness the sun shone on Siena, and, that all her houses, overtowered by the graceful La Mangia and the tall *Duomo Campanile*, glistened in the bright light.

About five miles from the city the desolation was somewhat relieved, for there were hedges by the roadside, and beyond, sloping olive-gardens and vineyards. Poplars grew by little streams, and sometimes we rode under oaks. On the top of every grey hill, giving it colour, was a farmhouse, rows of brilliant pumpkins laid on its red walls, ears of yellow corn hung in its *loggia*, and gigantic haystacks standing close by. There were monasteries too, great square brick buildings with tall towers, and below, spire-like cypresses. But between the farms and fertile fields were deep ravines and dry beds of streams. The road was lonely. Now and then flocks of birds flew down in front of the tricycle, or large white geese came out from under the hedge and hissed at us. For a few minutes a man driving a donkey-cart made the way not a little lively. He did not see us until we wheeled by him. Then he jumped as if he had been shot. "Dio!" he exclaimed, "but you frightened me!" He laughed, however, and whipping up his donkey rattled after us as if eager for a race, talking and shouting all the while and until we were out of hearing. One or two peasants passed in straw, chariot-shaped wagons, and once from a farmhouse a woman in red blouse and yellow apron, with a basket on her head and a dog at her heels, came towards us. It was at this same farm-house we met a Didymus.[55] We stopped as we had a way of doing when anything pleased us; and he came out to have a better look at the *tramvai*.[56] And how far did we expect to go to-day? he asked. To Monte Oliveto, J— told him, for, like pious pilgrims, we thought to make a day's retreat with the monks there. "To Monte Oliveto! and in a day, and on that machine!" and he laughed us to scorn. "In a week, the *Signore* had better say." Later a stone-breaker's belief in us made some amends for the farmer's contempt. We were riding then. "*Addio!*"[57] he cried, even before we reached him.

I shall always remember a little village through which we rode that morning because it was there we saw the first large stone-pine growing by the roadside which showed we were getting further south, and because of the friendliness of a peasant. It was a poor place. The people were ragged and squalid and sickly as if the gloom of the hills had fallen upon them. We asked at a shop for a lemon, but there was not one to be had. "Wait," cried a woman standing close by and she disappeared. She returned almost immediately with a lemon, on whose stem there were still fresh green leaves. "*Ecco!*" she said, "it is from my garden." "How much?" asked J— as she handed it to him. "Oh, nothing, sir," and she put her hands behind her back. We made her take a few coppers, for the children, we told her. As far as it lay in her power, I think she was as courteous as those men in a certain Italian town, who, in days long past, fought together for the stranger who came within their gates, so eager were they all not to cheat him, as is the way with modern landlords, but to lodge him at their own expense, so that there were no inns in that town.

Before we reached Buonconvento the clouds rolled away and the sun came out. It had rained here earlier in the morning. The roads were sticky and the machine ran heavily, and trees and hedges were wet with sparkling raindrops. There is an imposing entrance to the little town—a pointed bridge over a narrow stream, with a Madonna and Child in marble relief at the highest point, an avenue of tall poplars with marble benches set between, and then the heavy brick walls, blackened with age, and the gateway, its high Gothic arch decorated with the old Sienese wolf,[58] and a more recent crop of weeds.

We rode from one end to the other—a two minutes' ride—without finding a trattoria. At length we appealed to the crowd. Where was the *trattoria*? No one understood, and yet that very morning J— had been asked if he were not a Florentine. "Perhaps *Monsieur* speaks French?" and a little Frenchman in seedy clothes jauntily worn, and with an indescribable swagger, came forward, hat in hand. The effect of his coming was magical. For unknown reasons, when it was found that J— could speak French after a fashion, his Italian was all-sufficient. The *albergo* was here; we were directly in front of it, and the *padrone*, who had been at our elbows all the time, led the way into it. The Frenchman gallantly saw us through the crowd to the room where we were to dine. It was the best *trattoria* in the place, but poor enough, he said. Such bread and cheese! horrible! and he shrugged his shoulders and raised his hands to heaven in testimony thereof. He did not live in Buonconvento, not he. He came from Paris. Then he complimented J— on his Italian, to make up in some measure for the failure of the people to appreciate it, and with a bow that might have won him favour at court, and a "I salute you, *Monsieur* and Madame" he politely left us before our dinner was served. He was a strolling actor, the *padrone* said; he and his troupe would give a performance in the evening.

The fact that we were going to Monte Oliveto annoyed the *padrone*. The monastery is a too successful rival to his inn. Few travellers except those who are on their way to Monte Oliveto pass through his town, and few who can help it stay there over night. His list of the evils we should have to endure was the sauce with which he served our beef-steak and potatoes. We must leave the post road for one that was stony and steep. Our *velocipede* could not be worked over it. It would take hours to reach the monastery, and we had better not be out after dark, for there were dangers untold by the way. But when he had said the worst he became cheerful, and even seemed pleased when we admired his kitchen, where brass and copper pots and pans hung on the walls, and where in one corner was a large fireplace with comfortable seats inside and a pigeon-house underneath. But when we complimented him on the walls of his town, Bah! he exclaimed, of what use were they? They were half destroyed. They would be no defence in war times.

He was right. The walls, strong by the gate, have in parts entirely dis-appeared, and in others houses and stables have been made of them. It is on the open space by these houses that the men have their playground. They were all there when we arrived, and still there when we left. Young men, others old enough to be their fathers, and boys were, each in turn, holding up balls to their noses, and then, with a long slide and a backward twist of the arm, rolling them along the ground, which is the way Italians play bowls.[59]

Before the afternoon was over we cursed in our hearts the Tuscan politeness we had heretofore praised. About a mile from Buonconvento the road to Monte Oliveto divided. We turned to the right. But two peasants with ox-teams called out from below that we must not go that way. It was all bad. But to the left it was good, and *piano*,⁶⁰ ascending but gently, and we had much better take it. In an evil moment we did. That it ill behoves a wise man to seek counsel in every word spoken to him we found to our cost. In the first place the ascent was not gentle; we had not then learned that an Italian calls every hill that is not as straight up and down as the side of a house, piano. And in the second place the road was not good, but vilely bad. Unfortunately for half a mile, or perhaps more, it was fair enough. But when we had gone just so far that we were unwilling to turn back, we discovered our mistake. The road we had not taken was that built by the monks hundreds of years ago; we had chosen the new and not yet finished by-way. It was heavy with dust and dirt, and full of ruts and loose stones. Over it we could not ride or even push the tricycle without difficulty. It was in keeping, however, with the abomination of desolation lying on each side. For we were now in a veritable wilderness, a land of deserts and of pits where few men dwelt. All around us were naked, colourless chalk hills, abrupt precipices and ravines. A few chestnut trees, a rose bush covered with red berries growing from the grey earth were the only green things we passed for miles. It was weary and slow work, and the sun was low on the hill-tops before we came to the point where the two roads met. At some distance above us we saw a large red building surrounded by cypresses, and we knew this must be Monte Oliveto Maggiore. So we took heart again.

But our trouble was not over. The road was better only by comparison, and it was still impossible to ride, and hard work to push or pull the tricycle. It was made of bricks which lay as if they had been carelessly shot out of a cart and left where and when they fell. A little further on it divided again. A woman was walking towards us, and J— asked her which was the road to the convent—*il convento?* "You must go back," she said, "it lies miles below, Buonconvento." "These peasants are fools," said J— in angry English to her very face, but she, all unconscious, smiled upon us. We went to the left, which fortunately was just what we ought to have done. But it was provoking that, instead of getting nearer to the monastery we seemed to be going farther from it. With one turn of the road it appeared to be above, and with the next below us. Now it was on one side and now on the other, until I began to feel as if we were the answer

*Monte Oliveto.*

to the riddle I had so often been asked in my childhood, the mysterious "What is it that goes round and round the house but never gets in?" Soon the sun set behind the hills, and the sky grew soft and roseate. We met several peasants bearing large fagots of twigs on their heads. There were one or two shrines, a chapel, and a farm-house, in front of which a priest stood talking to a woman. But on we went without resting, J— pushing the machine and I walking behind, womanlike, shirking my share of the work. The road grew worse until it became nothing but a mass of ruts and gullies washed out by the rain, and led to a hill from which even Christian would have turned and fled. But we struggled up, reaching the top to see the gate of the monastery some sixty or seventy feet below. Finally we came to the great brick gateway which in the dull light, for by this time the colour had faded from the sky, rose before us a heavy black pile, beyond whose archway we saw only shadow and mystery. As we walked under it, our voices when we spoke were unnatural and hollow. On the other side the road wound through a gloomy grove of cypresses, growing so close together that they hedged us about with impenetrable darkness. Once several silent figures, moving noiselessly, passed by. Had we, by mischance, wandered into a Valley of the Shadow of Death?

The cypress grove, after several windings, brought us face to face with the building at which we had already so often looked from the distance. Even in the semi-darkness we could see the outline distinctly enough to know we were standing in front of the church, and that the detached building a little to our left was a barn or stable. But not a light shone in a window, not a doorway was in sight. I recalled my convent experience of bygone years,[61] and remembered that after eight o'clock in the evening no one was admitted within its walls. Was there a rule like this at Monte Oliveto, and was six the hour when its bolts and bars were fastened against the stranger? As we hesitated where to go or what to do next, three or four work-men came from the stable. J— spoke to them, and one offered to show him the entrance to the monastery while I waited by the tricycle. It was strange to stand in the late evening and in the wilderness alone with men whose speech I barely understood and whose faces I could not see. For fully five minutes I waited thus while they talked together in low voices. But at last I heard one cry. *Ecco!* here was the *padrone*; and they all took off their hats. A dog ran up and examined me, and then a man, who I could just make out in the gloom wore a cassock and the broad-brimmed priestly hat, joined the group. "*Buona sera*," he said to me. "Could I speak to him in French?" I asked. "Yes," he assented. "What was it I wanted?" When I told him we wished to stay in the monastery, he said he had not expected us. We had not written.

"But," I exclaimed, "we thought strangers were allowed to stay here."

"Yes," he answered; "there is a pension in the monastery; but it is for artists."

"And my husband is an artist," I interrupted eagerly, for from his manner I feared he would refuse us admission. After all, what did he know about us, except that, vagrant-like, we were wandering in the mountains at a most unseasonable hour? Indeed, when later I reflected on the situation, I realised that we must have seemed suspicious characters. At this critical moment J— returned. His guide had led him to a small side door beyond the church. There he had rung and rung again. The bell was loud and clear and roused many echoes within, but nothing else. The guide, perplexed, then led him back. I told him with whom I was speaking, and he continued the conversation with the *padrone*. Had they talked in Italian only or in French, they might have understood each other; but instead they used a strange mixture of the two, to their mutual bewilderment. If this kept on much longer we should undoubtedly spend the night in the open air. In despair I broke in, in French, "But, father, cannot we stay this one night?"

"Certainly," he said, fortunately dropping all Italian. "That is what I was explaining to Monsieur. You can stay, but of course we have nothing prepared. We will do our best."

If he had said he would do his worst, provided we were rid of the tricycle for the night, and were ourselves indoors where we might sit down, we should have been thankful.

The bags were unstrapped and given into the care of one of the men, a place was made for the machine in the stable, and then we followed the *padrone* or *Abate*—for this was his real title—to the door where J— had rung in vain, and which he opened with his key. Within it was so dark that we groped our way through the hall and a small cloister. Then we came to a flight of steps where, at the bidding of the *Abate*, as if to reassure us that we were not being led to secret cells or torture chambers, the man carrying our bags struck a solitary match. By this feeble light we walked up the broad stone stairs, and through many passage-ways, not a sound breaking the stillness but our steps and their loud echoes, to a door where the *Abate* left us, and at the same time the match burnt out. But the next minute he reappeared with a lighted taper, and at the end of the hall opened another door, lit a lamp on a table within, and showed us four rooms, which, he said, were at our disposal. The beds were not made, but they would be attended to immediately. He had now to say Office, but at nine supper would be served. Here was a very comfortable solution to the mystery into which the massive gateway seemed to lead. The Valley of the Shadow of Death had turned out to be a Delectable Land.[62]

It was still more comfortable later, when, his Office said, the *Abate* came back and sat and talked with us. Now he could examine us by a better light, I think he concluded we were not dangerous characters, probably only harmless lunatics. However that may be, after half an hour when the supper-bell rang, and we started off for the refectory, again by the light of his taper, we were the best of friends. The long corridor, thus dimly seen, seemed interminable. We went down one staircase, to find the door locked against us, then up and down another. Here the light went out, leaving us in a darkness like unto that of Egypt. The *Abate* laughed as if it was the best of jokes. He took J—'s hand and J— took mine, and thus like three children we went laughing down the staircase, and along more passages, and at last into a long refectory, at the further end of which was a lamp, while a door, to one side of that by which we entered, opened, and a second monk in white robes, holding a lighted taper, came in, and when he saw us made a low bow. As there were no other visitors, we were to eat with him and his brother monk, the *Abate* said; and then he gave me the head of the table, asking me if I were willing to be the Lady Abbess.

If we had been two prodigals, he could not have been kinder than he was, now he had given us shelter. If we had been starving like the hero of the parable, he could not have been more anxious to set before us a feast of plenty. Nor would any fatted calf have been more to our taste than the substantial supper prepared for us. We must eat, he said. We needed it. He had seen us coming up the hill as he talked with a peasant by the roadside. But *Monsieur* was push-pushing the machine and looking at nothing else, and *Madame* was panting and swinging her arms, staring straight in front of her; and before he had time to speak we had passed. We must drink too. The wine was good for us. We must not mix water with it. It was Christian; why then should it be baptised? The White Brother[63] spoke little, but he never allowed J—'s plate to remain empty. When the meat was brought in we were joined by Pirro, a good sized dog with no tail to speak of, and Lupo, an unusually large cat, and his numerous family, who all had to be fed at intervals. But even while Pirro jumped nimbly into the air after pieces of bread thrown to him, and Lupo scratched, and his progeny made mournful appeals to be remembered, and we talked, I looked every now and then down the long, narrow table to where it was lost in deep shadow. The cloth was laid its entire length, as if in readiness for the banished brothers whenever they might return. I should not have been surprised then to see the door open to admit a procession of white monks, all with tapers in their hands. The *Abate* must have realised that to a stranger there was something uncanny in his dark, silent, deserted monastery, and his last word as he bade us good-night was that we were to fear nothing, but to sleep in peace.

## Monte Oliveto[64]

The days we spent at Monte Oliveto were golden days. For we not only slept there one, but several nights, and the *Abate* declared we could remain as long as we might care to. Nothing could be more melancholy and wild than the country into which we had come. It is the most desolate part of all that strange desolation which lies to the south-east of Siena. The mountain on which the monastery is built is surrounded on every side but one by deep, abrupt ravines. Behind it rise higher mountains, bare and bleak and grey, like gigantic ash-piles, and on the very highest peak is the wretched little village of Chiusure. The other hills around are lower, and from the road by the convent gateway one can see Siena, pale and blue on the horizon, and southward, over

*Chiusure.*

the barren hill-tops, Monte Amiata. But Monte Oliveto with its gardens and orchards and vineyards, is a green place in the midst of the barrenness. The mountain sides are terraced, and olives and vines grow almost to the bottom of the ravine. It was said in old times that the Bishop of Arezzo was commanded in a vision to call the monastery after the Mount in Jerusalem. Nowadays sceptics say the trees on the terraces explain the name, forgetting that in the beginning this hill was as bare as the others. Why cannot it be believed for the legend's sake that the olives were planted afterwards because of the name?

The first morning the *Abate* took us to see the frescoes representing the life of St. Benedict, painted on the walls of the large cloister. I will be honest, and confess that they disappointed us. I doubt whether the artists were very proud of them. Luca Signorelli,[65] before he had finished the first side of the cloister, gave up the work, as it is not likely he would have done had he cared much for it. Sodoma,[66] when he took his place, was at first so careless that the then abbot took him to task, but the artist calmly told him more could not be expected for the price that was paid him. Certainly with neither were these frescoes a labour of love, and this one feels at once. One wonders if this could have been the same Sodoma who painted the St. Sebastian in Florence, and yet there is more charm in his pictures than in those of Signorelli. But what I cared for most were his portraits of himself, with heavy hair hanging about his face, and wearing the cloak the Milanese gentleman, turned monk, had given him, and of his wife and child; and the pictures of the raven and the other pets he brought with him to the monastery, to the wonder of the good monks.

It is a pity every one cannot look at these frescoes with such loving, reverential eyes as the *Abate*. He had shown them probably to hundreds of visitors; he had seen them almost every day for the many years he had been at Monte Oliveto; but his pleasure in them was as fresh as if it dated but from yesterday. He told the story of each in turn—of how in this one the great St. Benedict put the devil to flight, and how in that he, by a miracle, recalled an erring brother; and once he pointed to a palm-tree in a background. Sodoma, he said, had seen and admired a palm in the garden of the monastery, and so, after his realistic fashion, had painted it in just as he had his pets. That very tree was in the garden still. He would show it to us if we liked.

There never was such another garden! It is close to the large brick house or palace by the gateway, where in old times lay visitors were lodged, and beyond which no woman was ever allowed to pass. It is small, but in it the monks only raised the rarest trees and plants. Here grew the precious herbs out of which in the pharmacy, whose windows overlooked the quiet green inclosure, they prepared the healing draughts for which people came from far and near. The pharmacy is closed now. There is dust in the corners and on the quaint old chairs. Cobwebs hang from the ceiling. But brass scales are still on the heavy wooden counter, and pestle and mortar behind it, and glass retorts of strange shapes in the corners and above the doors. Majolica jars,[67] all marked with the three mountains, the cross and olive-branch, the *stemma* of the monastic order, are ranged on the brown shelves, many of the large ones carefully sealed, while from the smaller come forth strange odours of myrrh and incense and rare ointments. As in the refectory, everything here is in order for the monks when they return. But they will find more change in the garden below. The rare plants, the ebony and the hyssop, the cactuses and the palm, which made us think even less of Sodoma's frescoes than we had before, the pomegranates and the artichokes, are all there. But weeds grow in the paths, and by the old grey well, and in among the herbs; roses have run riot in the centre of the garden and turned it into a wild, tangled growth. To us it seemed the loveliest spot in Monte Oliveto. The hours spent in it were like a beautiful idyl of Theocritus or Shelley.[68] The sun shone and the air was filled with sweet spicy scents. To one side was the grey mountain, to the other dense cypresses, and above a blue, cloudless sky. The roses were still in bloom, and as we lingered there the *Abate* went from bush to bush, and picked for me a large bunch of fragrant buds. I hope if the monks ever do come back, that, while they throw open the windows of the pharmacy and let the light in again upon the majolica and the dark wood-work, they will leave the gates of the garden locked. It is fairer in its confusion than it ever could be with weeded paths and well-clipped bushes.

The *Abate* took us everywhere—through the empty guest-chambers of the palace to the tower, now a home for pigeons, from the top of which one has a wide view of the country, which, with its squares of olives and its grey hills and fields marked by deep furrows as if by boundary lines, looks like a large map or geological chart; through the monastery, with its three hundred rooms with now but three monks to occupy them; its cloisters, for there are two besides the large frescoed one; its *loggie*, where geraniums and other green plants were growing; its great refectory, beyond the door of which fowl or flesh meat never passed, and which is now used no longer; and its library, at the very top of the house, where rows of white vellum volumes are ready for the students who so seldom come. Then he led us to the church, where there are more altars than monks to pray before them, and a wonderful choir with inlaid stalls; and in and out of little chapels, one of which contains the grotto where blessed Bernardo Tolomei, the founder of the order, lived for many years after he came to the wilderness, while another was the first church used by the brotherhood, and the Virgin with angels playing to her on harps and mandolines, above the altar, was painted long before Signorelli and Sodoma began their work. Then there was the lemon-grove to be seen, where the *Abate* filled our pockets with the ripe fruit, which we were to keep, he said, in case we might be thirsty on the road some day when there was no wine or water near by to drink. And after that there was still to be visited the wine-press, with its deep shadows, and dark corners, and long subterranean passage to the room below, where men were filling small casks from large butts and then carrying them off on their shoulders to be weighed and stored above. We had to taste the wine, and I think it, together with the sunshine and the flowers, must have gone to our heads that morning and stayed there so long as we were at Monte Oliveto, for everything about us seemed to belong less to the actual world than to a dreamland full of wonder and beauty and sometimes of pathos.

It was the same in the afternoon, when the *Abate* had gone about his work—for he is a busy man, like the centurion with many under him—and J— and I wandered alone over the grey hills up to Chiusure. Life with its hardships must be real enough to the people of this little village, in which seeds of pestilence, sown hundreds of years ago, still bear the bitter fruit of wretchedness. It seems as if the brick walls which could not keep out the plague have ever since successfully barred the way to all prosperity, for generation after generation is born within them but to live and die in poverty. We saw melancholy figures there, old hags of women, with thin white hair and bent almost double under heavy bundles of wood, toiling up steep, stony streets with bare feet, and others crouching in the gloom opposite open doorways. Even the little priest, who, in his knee-breeches and long frock-coat and braided smoking-cap with tassels dangling in his eyes, humorous enough to look at, was pathetic in his way. For, after he had shown us his church with its decorations, poor as the people who worship in it, and offered us a glass of wine in his own parlour, he spread on the table before us some broken pieces of glass easily put together, on which a picture was painted. Was it of value? he asked, so eagerly that he told without further words the story of wants but ill supplied. He was willing to sell it, but he did not know what it was worth. Could we tell him? No, we could not, we said, for we really knew nothing about it, though we feared the hopes he had set upon it would never be realised. And then sadly he gathered together the pieces and put them away again in their newspaper wrapping.

It was more cheerful outside the gateway. There, in the late afternoon, the grey olives by the way were more clearly defined against the sky, and the grey ravines below more indistinct. Beyond, the hills, now all purple and soft, rolled away to the horizon and to the brilliant red sky above. One or two lights were lit in distant farm-houses, and once we heard a far-off bell. Before us the white road led by one green hill on whose top was a circle of cypresses, and in its centre a black cross, as in so many old pictures. But the strangest part of this dream-life was the friendship that sprang up between us and the monks. I should not have been more surprised if St. Benedict and Blessed Bernardo had come back to earth to make friends with us. It was not only that the *Abate* acted as our guide through the monastery. This he does for every visitor who comes, since the Government took possession of it and turned it into a public art gallery and pension for artists. But he came to our room early in the morning to drink his coffee with us, and in the evening, after he had said his Office, for a little talk. And when we had finished our supper we sat together long over our wine, talking now in French, now in English, now in Italian, and occasionally understanding each other. Like all good fellows, we too had our jokes. But the *Abate*'s favourite was to tell how he had seen us coming up the mountain, *Monsieur* push-pushing the *velocipede* and *Madame* puff-puffing behind him. Even Dom Giuseppe, the other monk—the third was away—relaxed from the dignity with which he had first met us, and took part in the talk and the laughter. Unreal as seemed these late suppers in the long refectory, in the dim light, with Pirro for ever jumping after choice morsels while Lupo and his family growled with rage and envy from under the table, we strayed even farther into Wonderland[69] the second day after our arrival, when both monks went out for a ride on the tricycle along the mulberry walk and by Blessed Bernardo's grotto.

The last day of our stay a number of visitors arrived—a priest from Perugia, two nuns, and two English ladies. They were not expected, and dinner had to be prepared for them. The *Abate* is never pleased when guests come without giving him warning. When we met him in the refectory a little after twelve, we could see his patience had been tried. We must pardon him for being late, he said, but he had had to find something to eat for all these people. Were they to dine with us? we asked. No, indeed, was his answer. They were not members of the community. This confirmed our doubts as to whether we might not be monks without our knowing it; for the first morning the *Abate* had given us a key of the great front door, by which we could let ourselves in at all hours, without any ringing of bells or calling of porters, so that we felt as if we belonged to the convent. These visitors were the thorns in his present life, the *Abate* continued, and we were his roses. Then he brought out a bottle of the *vino santo* which he makes himself, and prizes so highly that he never sells it as he does the other wines, and a plate of grapes for which he had sent a great distance. And when dinner was over he bade the servant put all that was left of grapes and wine away. They were for the community, and not for common folk. He introduced us to the Perugian priest, who might possibly, he said, be of use to us in Perugia. The latter almost embraced J— in his protestations of good-will, and came running back several times to press his hand, and say in a French of his own invention that we must call often during our stay in his city.

## Through the Wilderness to a Garden

We left the monastery the next morning. It took courage on our part. But we knew it was best to go quickly. Every day we fell more under the dreamy influence of the place and became less willing for action. We must hasten from Monte Oliveto, for the very reason which led Blessed Bernardo to it—to flee temptation. The *Abate* was in our room by half-past seven. Dom Giuseppe was in the church saying mass, but had sent his farewells. He himself had not yet said mass, so he could not drink his coffee with us, but he sat by while we had ours. We should not reach San Quirico till noon, he feared, and we must have something in our pockets to eat in the meantime, and he went to his room and came back with two cakes. He brought besides two letters he had written introducing us to monks at San Pietro in Perugia. Then he came down stairs and out to the stable, though he was fasting, and the morning was wet and cloudy and cold. We did not get on the tricycle at once. We remembered the road too well. The *Abate* walked by our side, now and then patting J— on the back and calling him affectionately "Giuseppe, Giuseppe," and kept with us until, at some little distance from the gateway, we mounted the machine. After he had said good-bye he stood quietly watching us. Then there came a turn in the road which hid him from us, and when we saw him again he was walking on the foot-path below the cypresses, with two little boys who had come out with him. He was on his way to take Dom Giuseppe's place at the altar. And then we went on sadly, for we knew that we should not come to another resting-place where there was such perfect relief for pilgrims that are weary and faint in the way.

As the road was difficult going up, so was it dangerous coming down, and again we had to walk. To add to our discomfort, before long it began to rain, and it was so cold we had to blow on our fingers to keep them warm. During the night it had snowed on the far mountain ranges. Beyond Buonconvento, when we returned to the post-road, we went fast enough, but only for a while. There were more mountains to cross, up which J— could not go very fast because of the burden, or knapsack, that was on his back. Out of very shame I took my share in pushing and pulling the tricycle. Once or twice we had long coasts; but in places the road was sandy, and in descending wound as often as a small St. Gothard Railway.[70] Coasting would have been too great a risk, especially as I never could begin back-pedalling going down hill, though on up-grades but too often, J— complained, that like Dante on the hill-side[71] my firm foot ever was the lower! The way still lay between and over hills of chalk, and we rode for miles through monotonous barrenness. It rained at intervals, but at times the sun almost broke through the clouds which followed it in long grey sweeps from the white masses on the snow-capped mountains bounding the horizon. To our right, Monte Amiata, bare and rugged and with white top, was always in sight, and once, above it, the clouds rolled away, leaving a broad stretch of greenish-blue sky. There were many crosses by the wayside, and they were different from any we had yet seen. On each, above spear and sponge, was a black cock, rudely carved to look as if it were crowing. Just before we came to San Quirico, and towards noon, we saw at the foot of one of these crosses an old, weary-looking peasant, with head bowed, as if he listened for the Angelus.

We were prepossessed against San Quirico before we reached it. Olives with vines hanging from them, in defiance of Virgil,[72] brown fields, and red and yellow trees could not reconcile us to the long climb up the mountain. It was worth our trouble, however, if only to see the cathedral. We left the tricycle at the *trattoria*, and at our leisure looked at the portal and its pillars, with quaintly carved capitals of animals and birds, and those others, joined together with a Celtic- like twist and resting on leopards, and the two sea-monsters above. And while we looked at the grotesque gargoyles on the walls, and the two figures for columns, and the lions on the side doorway, two *carabinieri* from a neighbouring window examined us as if we were equal curiosities. This fine building is an incongruity in San Quirico, which—for our first impressions proved right—is at best but a poor place. We were cheated in it as we had never been before. When we went back to the *trattoria* four men were eating their dinner inside the fire-place in the kitchen. But we were ushered into what I suppose was the best room. It was dining-room and bed-chamber combined. On one side was a long table, on the other the bed. The dressing-table served as buffet, and the *padrona* brought from its drawers the cheese and apples for our dessert. In the garden below, for we were in the second story, weeds like corn grew so tall that they shaded the window. What happened in that room, and the difference that arose between the *padrona* and ourselves, are facts too unpleasant to recall! But I am sure the next foreigners who went to San Quirico heard doleful tales of the evil doings of the two *Inglesi* who came on a *velocipede*.

After San Quirico there was the same barrenness, and only indifferent roads over rolling country. Until within half a mile of Pienza, where the hedges began again, not a tree grew by the roadside, and the only signs of vegetation were the reeds in the little dark pools dotting the grey fields. It was still bitterly cold, and my fingers tingled on the handles. Once we passed a farmhouse where a solitary woman watched a herd of black swine, and once we met the diligence.[73] That was all.

We rode into Pienza, though our way lay to one side of it. But we were curious to see the cathedral and palaces Pius II. built there, in the fond hope of turning his native village into an important town. Of all the follies of proud popes I think this was the greatest. As well might he have hoped by his single effort to cover the *creta*, or chalk, with roses as to raise a prosperous city in its midst. We saw the great brown buildings marked with the five crescents of the Piccolomini and the papal tiara and keys, as out of place in Pienza as the cathedral seemed in San Quirico; we looked closer at the old stone well and its beautiful wrought iron work. J— made a sketch of a fine courtyard, and then we were on the road again.

Near Montepulciano we came to a thickly wooded country, riding for several miles between chestnuts and oaks. There were open places too, from which we saw far below the fair Val di Chiana, and in the distance Lake Thrasymene, pale and silvery; and close by olive gardens, through whose grey branches we looked at the purple mountains and their snowy summits. Above were broad spaces of bright sky, for the dark clouds were rolling away beyond the lake, and those that floated around Monte Amiata were now glistening and white. We had left the wilderness for a garden. All the bells rang out a welcome when, after working up the long road—so winding that at times the city was completely hidden—we wheeled into the now dark and cold streets of Montepulciano.

### The Pilgrims are Detained in Montepulciano

It was in this high hill town that one of the pilgrims fell by the way. For two days J— was too ill to ride, and we feared our pilgrimage had come to an end. We stayed at the Albergo Marzocco, whose praises Mr. Symonds has sung.[74] It was on the fifth floor of an old palace, and the entrance was through the kitchen. The *padrone* and his family were very sociable. Almost immediately his wife wanted to know the trade of the *Signore*. "Ah! an artist. Eccomi! I am a washer-woman!" She was also cook. From the dining-room we could watch her as she prepared our meals. When she kept us waiting too long we had only to step into the kitchen and stand over her until the dish we had ordered was ready. We could look too into an adjacent room, where during our stay one daughter of the house for ever ironed table-cloths, while a second added up endless accounts.

But friendly as these people were, they were stupid. The *padrone* had a *pizzicheria*, or pork shop, across the street. When anything was wanted at the inn, it was brought from the shop. Every time I went to my window I saw messengers on their way between the two establishments. But no man can serve two masters. The *pizzicheria* drove a more thriving trade and the inn suffered in consequence. It was left in the charge of a youth of unparalleled stupidity, who seldom understood what we asked for, and when he did declared it something not to be had. But a friend was sent to us in our need.

It happened in this way. The first morning we went out for a walk. As we started a harlequin, newly painted in red and white, struck nine from a house-top near by. In the Via dell' Erbe, women, their heads covered with gay handkerchiefs or wide-brimmed, high-crowned felt hats, were selling vegetables and fruit. Just in front of us were three beggars, two blind and one lame, walking hand in hand, and an old brown monk with a wine cask on his shoulder. At almost every turn we saw through an archway the three far away lakes of Montepulciano, Chiusi and Thrasymene. But it was now J— began to feel ill, and we went into a *caffè* and called for cognac. As we sat there the door opened, and a young Italian dressed *à l'Anglaise*, even to his silver-headed cane, came in. He took a seat at the table next to us. When his coffee was brought in he asked the waiter if he had seen the English lady and gentleman who had arrived the evening before on a *velocipede*. No, the *cameriere* had not; he knew nothing of these *forestieri*. There was a pause while the young Italian sipped his coffee. But presently he turned to us and said in good English, but with a marked accent:

"I beg pardon, sare, but was it not you who came to Montepulciano on a tricycle?"

"Yes," J— said, rather curtly.

"Ah, I thought so!" the Italian continued, well satisfied with the answer. "I have seen it—a Humber.[75] It is a beautiful machine. I myself do ride a bicycle, the *Speecial Cloob*.[76] You know it? I do belong to the *Cyclists' Touring Cloob*, and to the *Speedvell Cloob*. All the champions belong to that *Cloob*. I did propose some one for director at the last meeting; you will see my name on that account in the papers. Here is my card, but in the country around Montepulciano all call me Sandro or Sandrino. I have ridden from Florence to Montepulciano in one day. I have what you call the wheel-fever," and he smiled apologetically and stopped, but only to take breath.

We were fellow-cyclers and that was enough. We were friends at once, though J— was too ill to be enthusiastic, and though our record would have disgusted the *Speedvell Cloob*. He was sorry J— was not well. He could sympathise. He was feeling *vary bad* himself, because the day before he had gone on his bicycle as far as Montalcino with a gun to *keel the little birds*. It was too far even for a champion. But he had taken the waters—Janos—he had great faith in the waters. The cognac had by this time made J— better, and we started to leave the *caffe*. Sandrino, to give him his Montepulciano name, insisted on paying for everything. We must let him have that favour, he said, and also another. He was not a native of the town. He was a Roman, as he supposed we could see by his nose. But still he would like to do us the honours of the place. He would take us to see so fine a church. We could not but be pleased with it. It was only a step. Foolishly we went. The step was a long one. It took us half way down the mountain-side to the Madonna di San Biagio. But J— was now really too wretched to look at anything, and we turned back at once. As we walked slowly up again Sandrino explained that he had lived in England several years, and it turned out that he had the English as well as the wheel fever. All his clothes were from London, he said. He smoked English tobacco. A friend sent it to him, and he showed us the small paper box tied with a string in which he kept it. And most of his news was English, too. His friends wrote him. He had just had a letter—see—and he opened it. There had been fearful riots in England. He cared much for the politics of the country. But the refrain to all he said was praise of cycling. He offered to ride with us when we left Montepulciano. He could go any day but the next, which was his twenty-first birthday, and when he was to have a great dinner and many friends and much wine. He would call, if we would allow him, and with profession of great friendship he left us at the door of the inn.

He was true to his word. Indeed, I do not know what had become of us but for his kindness. We were both depressed by this unlooked-for delay, and he not only helped to amuse but was of practical use to us. He came twice the following day. The first time he stopped, he said, to tell us he did hear from friends in Castiglione del Lago, who, if we would ride to-morrow, would be glad to see us at lunch. "There will be nothing much," he concluded. "They will make no preparations. We just take whatever they have. It will be some leetle thing." Though in the first glory of his twenty-one years, he went with me to a druggist's to act as interpreter. But I think he was repaid by his pleasure in carrying back a bottle of his favourite waters. The *cameriere*,[77] when he saw it, with his usual cleverness followed into the room with three glasses. If we had asked for three, he would have brought one. Sandrino's second visit was in the evening, after he had eaten his great dinner and drunk much wine, which had again made him feel *vary bad*. Had we ever tasted the famous Montepulciano, "king of all wine"? he asked. No? Well, we must before leaving the town. It was not to be had in the shops. He had been presented with many bottles. He repeated his invitation to lunch in Castiglione, and it seemed that other friends in a villa near Cortona would also be charmed to see us, and to give us wine if we were tired.

## In the Val di Chiana

The next morning J— was much better, and we decided to ride. Sandrino arrived at half-past seven and breakfasted with us. In the uniform of the *Speedvell Cloob*, its monogram in silver on his cap, he was even more English than he had been the day before. Our last experience at the *albergo* was characteristic. The *cameriere*, overcome by Sandrino's appearance, became incapable of action. We called for our coffee and rolls in vain. Finally, we all, our guest included, made a descent upon the kitchen and forced him to bestir himself.

It was Sunday morning, and the news of our going had been noised abroad. The aristocracy as well as the people turned out to see us off. Many of Sandrino's friends lingered in the barber's shop across the street. Others waited just without the city gate with his mother and sister. When Sandrino saw the crowd he sprang upon his *Speecial Cloob*, worked with one foot and waved the other in the air, rode to the little park beyond and back, and then jumped off, hat in hand, at his mother's side, with the complacent smile of a champion. Indeed, the whole ride that day savoured of the circus. He went down hills with his legs stretched straight out on either side. On level places he made circles and fancy figures in the road. Whenever we passed peasants—and there were many going to church—he shrieked a warning, shrill as a steam-engine whistle. No wonder he said he had no use for a bell! He spoke to all the women, calling them his "beautiful cousins." And in villages the noise he made was so great that frightened people, staring at him, never looked behind, so that several times we all but rode over men and women who walked backward right into our wheels. And all the while J— like the ring-master, kept calling and shrieking, but no one paid the least attention to him.

Our way was through the beautiful Val di Chiana, no longer pestilential and full of stenches as in Dante's day, but fresh and fair, and in places sweet with clematis.[78] There were no fences or hedges, and it stretched from

*Leaving Montepulciano.*

mountains to mountains, one wide lovely park. About half way to Castiglione we came to the boundary line between Tuscany and Umbria, a canal with tall poplars on its banks, throwing long reflections into the water below, where a boat lay by the reeds. We stopped there some little time. Sandrino was polite, but I could see he did not approve. What would the *Speedvell Cloob* have thought? Farther on, when we loitered again, near a low farmhouse under the oaks, he wheeled quickly on. But presently he came back. "Oh," he said, "I thought you must have had an accident!"

There could be no lovelier lake town than Castiglione del Lago. The high hill on which it stands projects far into Lake Thrasymene. The olives, which grow from its walls down the hill-side into the very water, are larger and finer with more strangely twisted trunks than any I have ever seen. As we came near the town we rode between them, looking beneath their silvery-grey branches out to the pale blue quiet lake beyond. A woman came from under their shade with a bundle of long reeds on her head. A priest passed us on a donkey.

We left our machines in a stable at the foot of the hill, and walked through the streets. Here Sandrino's invitation came to nought. His friends were away. Whatever *leetle thing* we had must be found elsewhere. So we went to a *trattoria*, where another of his friends, a serious, polite young man, who, we learned afterwards, owns the town and all the country thereabouts, sat and talked with us while we ate our lunch. Poor Sandrino! He had to pay for his English clothes and foreign friends! The *padrona*, backed by the *padrone* from the kitchen below, asked him no less than five francs for our macaroni and wine. A dispute, loud because of the distance between the disputants, followed; but in the end Sandrino paid four francs, though half that sum would have been enough. It was some consolation for us to know that we, *forestieri*,[79] had never been cheated so outrageously.

It was pleasant wandering through the town, with the grave young man as guide, to the Palazzo Communale, where the red and white flag of the Duke of Cornia waving outside was the same as that painted in the old frescoes within, and where councilmen, holding council, bowed to us as we passed; and then to the old deserted castle which, with its grey battlemented walls and towers, was not unlike an English ruin. But it was pleasanter when, Sandrino having kissed his friend, we were on the road again, riding between yellow mulberries by the side of the lake. Sheep were grazing on the grassy banks. Donkeys and oxen were at rest in the meadows. But the peasants, mass heard, were at work again. Women on ladders were stripping the mulberries of their leaves; men on their knees were digging in the fields.

At the villa, Sandrino's friends were at home. At the gate the gay bicycler gave his war-cry. A young lady ran out between the roses and chrysanthemums in the garden and by the red wall where yellow pumpkins were sunning, to welcome him. Then her mother and sister came and also gave him greeting. They received us with courtesy. We were led into the drawing-room, a bare, barn-like place with cold brick floor, where there were three or four chairs, a table, an old piano, faded cretonne curtains hung on rough sticks at the windows, and small drawings pinned on the wall. A man in blue coat and trousers, such as the peasants wear, followed us in and sat down by the young ladies. He was one of her men, the *Signora* explained, and this was a house she had rented for the summer. Then we had the wine Sandrino promised, and we became very friendly. One of the daughters knew a little English, but when we spoke to her she hid her face in her hands and laughed and blushed. She never, never would dare to say a word before us, she declared. She was very arch and girlish. One minute she played a waltz on the piano; the next she teased Sandrino, and there was much pleasantry between them. The mother spoke French after a fashion, but when she had anything to say she relapsed into Italian. She lived in Rome, she said. We must come and see her there. But would we not now stay at her villa all night, instead of in Cortona? Then she squeezed my hand. "*Vous êtes bien sympathique!*"[80] she said, and I think she meant to compliment me. Her husband, it seems, was a banker in Rome,

*On the Hill.*

and would be pleased, so she told us through Sandrino's interpretation, to do anything and everything for us.

Mother and daughters, men and maids, all walking amiably together, came to the garden-gate with us. The *Signora* here squeezed my hand a second time. The skittish young lady said "good-bye" and then hid behind a bush, and her sister gave us each some roses. It was here, too, we were to part with Sandrino. He must be in Montepulciano by six. More friends were coming. Would we write him postal cards to tell him of the distance and time we made? And that map of Tuscany we said we would give him, would we not remember it? He was going to take some great rides, and it would help him. Then we turned one way, and he, riding his best for the young ladies, the other, to be seen by us no more.

It was roses all the way to Cortona. They grew in villa gardens and along the road up the mountain; there were even a few among the olives, on the terraces whose stone supports make the city look from below as if it were surrounded by many walls instead of one only. Near the town we met two young lovers, their arms around each other's waists, and a group of men who directed us in our search for the inn up a short steep hill leading away from the main road. Above, inside the city gate, several other citizens told us we must go down again, for the road we had left led right by the door of the inn. Clearly the Albergo della Stella, for that was its name, was not well known in Cortona. After a climb of three miles it was provoking to go even a foot out of our way, and we turned back in no cheerful mood. It was disheartening, when, having come to the inn, we found the lower floor, by which we entered, the home of pigs and donkeys and oxen. The Major was right, I thought; Cortona was a rough place. The contrast when on the third floor of this establishment we were shown into a large clean really well-furnished room, with window overlooking the valley, made us neglect to drive a close bargain with the *padrona*, a neglect for which we suffered later.[81]

## Luca Signorelli's Town

The principal event of our stay in Cortona was a hunt for Luca Signorelli's house. Why we were so anxious to find it I did not know then, nor do I now; but we were very earnest about it. At the start a youth pursued us with the persistence of a government spy. It was useless to try and dodge him. No matter how long we were in churches or by what door we came out, he was always waiting in exactly the right place. In our indignation we would not ask him the way, but we did of some other boys, who forthwith led us such a wild-goose chase that I think before it was over there was not a street or corner of the town unvisited by us. We next employed an old man as guide. Of course he knew all about Luca Signorelli. He could show us all his frescoes and pictures in Cortona. Some of them were bad enough, as he supposed the *Signore* knew; they were painted in the artist's youth. But we wanted to see his house. Ah! we had but to follow him, and he led us in triumph to that of Pietro da Cortona. As this would not do, he consulted with an old woman who recommended a visit to a certain *padre*. The *padre* was in his kitchen. He had never heard of Signorelli's house, and honestly admitted his ignorance. But could he show us some fine frescoes or sell us antiquities? This failing, our guide hunted for some friends who, he declared, knew everything. But they were not in their shop, nor in the *caffè* nor on the *piazza*, and in despair he took us to see another priest. The latter wore a jockey-cap and goggles, and was a learned man. He had heard of a life of Signorelli by a German.[82] He had never read it, nor indeed could he say where it was to be had; but he knew there was such a book. He was certain our hunt was useless, since Signorelli had lived in so many houses the city could not afford to put tablets on them all, and so not one was marked. He himself was a professional letter-writer, and if the *Signore* had any letters he wished written—? We then gave up the search and dismissed the old man with a franc, though he declared himself still willing to continue it. It was in this way we saw Cortona.

*Cortona.*

For the last few days we had begun to be haunted by the fear of the autumn rains. If they were as bad as Virgil says,[83] and were to fall in dense sheets, tearing the crops up by the roots while black whirlwinds set the stubble flying and vast torrents filled ditches and raised rivers, the roads must certainly be made unrideable. Since the morning we left Monte Oliveto the weather had been threatening, and now in Cortona there were heavy showers. As we sat in our room at the *albergo* after our long tramp, and J— made a sketch from the window, we saw the sky gradually covered with dark clouds. The lake, so blue yesterday, was grey and dull. The valley and the mountains were in shadow, save where the sun, breaking through the clouds, shone on a small square of olives and spread a golden mist over Monte Amiata. Before J— had finished the gold faded into white and then deepened into purple, and we determined to be off early in the morning.

# To Perugia
BY TRAIN AND TRICYCLE

The next day I was tired and in no humour for riding. J— wanted once to try the tricycle without luggage over the Italian roads. It was settled then between us that I should go alone by train to Perugia, where we should meet. Before seven we had our breakfast and the *padrona* brought us her bill. Because we had not bargained in the beginning she overcharged us for everything, but we refused to pay more than was her due. There was the inevitable war of words, more unpleasant than usual because the *padrona*'s voice was loud and harsh and asthmatic. She grew tearful before it was over, but finally thanked us for what we gave her and asked us to come again so gently that we mistrusted her. I thought it as well to wait with the bags at the station, though my train did not start till eleven.

It was a beautiful coast down the mountain between the olives, four miles with feet up. The clouds had rolled away during the night, and it was bright and warm at the station when J— left me to go on his way. It was quiet, too, and for some time I was alone with the porters. But presently a young woman with a child in her arms, came by. She stopped and looked at me sympathetically. I spoke to her, and then she came nearer and patted me on the shoulder and said, "*Poverina!*"[84] It seems she had seen J— bring me to the station and then turn back by himself. I do not know what she thought was the trouble, but she felt sorry for me. She was the wife of the telegraph operator and lived in rooms above the station. She took me to them, and then she brought me an illustrated Italian translation of *Gil Blas*[85] to look at, while she made me a cup of coffee. Every few minutes she sighed and said again, "*Poverina!*" She gave me her card—Elena Olas, *nata* Bocci, was her name. I wrote mine on a slip of paper, and when the train, only an hour late, came, we parted with great friendship.

A regiment of soldiers was on its way to Perugia and made the journey very lively. Peasants, who had somehow heard of its coming, were in wait at every station with apples and chestnuts and wine, over which there was much noisy bargaining. At other times the soldiers sang. As the train carried us by the lake, from which the mountains in the distance rose white and shadowy and phantom-like; and by Passignano, built right in the water, with reeds instead of flowers around the houses, where fishermen were out in their boats near the weirs; and then by Maggiore and Ellora on their hill-tops, I heard the constant refrain of the soldiers' song, and it reminded me of my friend at Cortona, for it was a plaintive regret for "*Poverina mia.*" Then there came

*Piping down the Valley.*

a pause in the singing, and a voice called out, "*Ecco*, Perugia!" I looked from the carriage window, and there far above on the mountain I saw it, white and shining, like a beautiful city of the sun.

At the station J— met me. He had been waiting an hour, having made the thirty-six miles between Cortona and Perugia in three hours and a half. He had had his adventures too. Beyond Passignano he met a man on foot who spoke to him and to whom he said "*Buon giorno!*" "Good morning," cried the man in pure insular English, and J— in sheer astonishment stopped the tricycle. The tramp, for tramp he was, explained that he was an Englishman and in a bad way. He had been in Perugia with a circus which had had little or no success, and the rascally Frenchman who managed it, had broken it up and made off, leaving him with nothing. He was now on his way to Florence where he wanted to be taken on by Prince Strozzi who kept English jockeys.[86] But in the meantime he was hungry and had no money and must tramp it all the way. J— gave him a franc for his immediate wants. He looked at the money. He supposed he could get a little something with it, he grumbled. He really was grateful, however, for he offered to push the machine up a hill down which he had just walked. But J— telling him to hurry on, engaged instead the services of a small boy who was going his way. For pay he gave the child a coast down the other side into his native village, than which *soldi* could not have been sweeter. Did not all his play-mates see him ride by in his pride?

Arriving in Perugia, J— himself was a hero for a time. Many officers with their wives were in the station, and in their curiosity so far forgot their usual dignity as to surround him and beset him with questions as to his whence and whither, and what speed he could make. It is a long way from the station up the mountain to the town, but we went faster than we had ever climbed mountain before, for we tied the tricycle to the back of the diligence, J— rode and steered it, but I sat inside, ending my day's journey as I had begun it, in common-place fashion. The driver was full of admiration. We must go to Terni on our *velocipede*, he said, for in the mountains beyond Spoleto we would go down-hill for seven miles. *Ecco!* no need of a diligence then.[87]

## At Perugia

The *padrone* of the *albergo* at Perugia was a man of parts. He could speak English. When we complimented him on a black cat which was always in his office, he answered with eyes fixed on vacancy, and pausing between each word like a child saying its lesson: "Yes-it-is-a-good-cat. I-have-one-dog-and four-cats. This-cat-is-the-fa-ther-of-the-oth-er-cats. One-are-red-and-three-is-white." And when we had occasion to thank him, he knew enough to tell us we were very much obliged.

But we gave him small chance to display his powers. There was little to keep us in the inn when after a few minutes' walk we could be in the *piazza*, where the sun shone on Pisano's fountain, and on the palace of the Baglioni and the *Duomo* opposite. But what a fall was there! A couple of *gendarmes*, priests walking two by two, a few beggars, were the only people we saw in this broad *piazza*, where at one time men and women, driven to frenzy by the words of Fra Bernardino, spoken from the pulpit by the *Duomo* door, almost fell into the fire they had kindled to burn their false hair and ornaments, their dice and cards; and where at another, Baglioni fought, with the young Raphael looking on,[88] to paint later one at least of the combatants; and where the beautiful Grifonetto lay in death agony, the avengers of his murdered kinsmen waiting to see him die, the heads of his fellow assassins looking grimly down from the palace walls, and Atalanta, his mother, giving her forgiveness for the deed for which but yesterday she had cursed him. In the aisles of the *Duomo* once so stained with the blood of Baglioni that they had to be purified with wine before prayers could again be offered in them, a procession of white-robed priests and acolytes, bearing cross and censer, passed from one chapel to another before a congregation of two or three old women. It was the same in the narrow streets; all is now still and peaceful, where of old Baglioni, single-handed, kept back the forces of Oddi, their mortal foes. Only the memory of their fierceness and prowess remains; though I have two friends who say that in the dark street behind the palace, where brave Simonetto and Astorre[89] fought the enemy until corpses lay in piles around them, they one night heard voices singing sadly as if in lamentation; and these voices led them onwards under one archway and then another until suddenly the sounds ceased. But when they turned to go home-wards, lo! they had lost their way. The next morning they returned that they might by daylight see whence the music could have come. But all along the street was a blank wall. None but spirits could have sung there, and what spirits would dare to lift their voices in this famous street but those of Baglioni?

It must be the degeneracy of modern warriors that sets these heroes of the old school to singing lamentations. The Grifonettos and Astorres who feasted on blood, could they return to life and their native town, would have little sympathy with the captains and colonels who now drink tamarind water in the *caffe*, booted and spurred though the latter be. The *caffe* is everywhere the lounging-place of Italian officers, but in Perugia it seemed to be their headquarters. There was one on the Corso, a few doors from the palace, which they specially patronised. They were there in the morning even before the shops were opened, and again at noon, and yet again in the evening, while at other times they walked to and fro in front of it, as if on guard. But though the youngest as well as the oldest patronised it, the distinctions of rank between them were observed as scrupulously as Dickens says they are with the Chatham and Rochester aristocracy.[90] The colonel associated with nothing lower than a major, the latter, in turn, drawing the line at the captain, and so it went down to the third lieutenant, who lorded it only over the common soldier. On the whole I think the lesser officers had the best of it; for whether they ate cakes and drank sweet drinks, or played cards, they were always sociable and merry. Whereas, sometimes the colonel sat solitary in his grandeur, silent except for the few words with the boy selling matches as he hunted through the stock to find a box with a pretty picture.

We were long enough in Perugia to carry the *Abate*'s letters to San Pietro. The monks to whom, they were written were away, but a third came in their place and gave us to welcome. He showed J— the inner cloister, to which I could not go. Women were not allowed there. It was because of my skirts, he said; and yet he, too, wore skirts, and he spread out his cassock on each side. While they were gone I waited in the church. I wonder if ghostly voices are ever heard within it. The monks, long dead, whose love and even life it was to make it beautiful until its walls and ceilings were rich and glowing, its choir a miracle of carving, and its sacristy hung with prayer-inspiring pictures, have, like the Baglioni, cause to bewail the degenerate latter day. The beauty they created now lives but for the benefit of a handful of monks, whose monastery is turned into a Boys' Agricultural School, and for the occasional tourist. Later from the high terrace of the park opposite San Pietro we saw the boys in their blue blouses digging and hoeing in the fields under the olives, where probably the monks themselves once worked. There is in this little park an amphitheatre with an archway, bearing the Perugian griffin in the centre. It is shaded by dense ilex-trees, from whose branches a raven must once have croaked; for evil has come upon the place, as it has upon the grey monastery so near it. Instead of nobles and knights and men-at-arms and councillors of state, two or three poor women with their babies sat on the stone benches gossiping. And as we lingered there in the late afternoon there came from San Pietro the sound not of monks chanting vespers, but of some one playing the "Blue Danube" on an old jingling piano. Only the valley below, and the Tiber winding through it, and the mountains beyond are unchanged!

## Across the Tiber to Assisi

When we left Perugia in the early morning, we passed first by the statue of Julius II., thus receiving, we said to each other, the Bronze Pontiff's benediction. We imagined this to be an original idea; but it is useless to try to be original. Since then we have remembered the same thought came to Miriam and Donatello when they made the statue their trysting-place.[91] Then we rode through the *piazza*, where a market was being held, and where at one end a long row of women, all holding baskets of eggs, stood erect, though all around other women and even men, selling fruit and vegetables, sat comfortably on low stools. Out on the other side of the Porta Romana we saw that while Perugia was bright and clear in the sunlight, a thick white mist covered the valley, so that it looked as if a great lake, bounded by the mountains, lay below. The chrysanthemums and marigolds, hanging over high garden walls, and the grass by the roadside glistened with dew. Shining silver cobwebs hung on the hedges. Before many minutes, so fast did we go, we were riding right into the

*Perugia: The Bronze Pontiff's Benediction.*

mist. We could see but a few feet in front of us, and the olives on either side, through the heavy white veil, looked like spectres. We passed no one but a man carrying a lantern and a cage of owls. It seemed but natural that so uncanny a ride should lead to a home of shadows. And when we came to the tomb of the Volumnii at the foot of the mountain, we left the tricycle without, and went down for a while into its darkness and damp. When we came out the mist had disappeared and the road lay through sunshine.

A little farther on we had our first near view of the Tiber. We crossed it by the old Ponte San Giovanni, so narrow that there was not room enough for us to pass a boy and donkey just in front. J— called, and the boy pushed his donkey close to the stone wall; but for all that we could not pass. Even as he called he was stopped by a sudden pain in his side, the result probably of his descent into the tomb while he was still warm, for he had back-pedalled

*Assissi: A Frown of Disapproval.*

coming down the mountain. And so we waited many minutes on the bridge to see, not the yellow Tiber one always hears about, but a river blue in mid-stream, white where it came running over the mill-wheel and down the dam, and red and yellow and green where it reflected the poplars and oaks, and the skirts and handkerchiefs of the women washing on its banks. But after the bridge we left the river, for we were bound for Assisi. We had a quiet peaceful ride for several miles on the Umbrian plain, where in the old times no one dared to go without the permission of the Baglioni, between vineyards and fields where men were ploughing, and through insignificant little villages, and until we came out upon the large *piazza* in front of Santa Maria degli Angeli. It was crowded with peasants, for market was just over, and there came from every side the sound of many voices. When we rode by we were surrounded at once, two or three men keeping close to our side to sing the praises of the hotels at Assisi and shower their cards upon us. They pursued us even into the church and as far as the little hermitage beneath the dome, to tell us that each and all could speak English.

If the Umbrians about Assisi were always like this, Saint Francis was a wise man to hide himself in the woods and to make friends with beasts and birds. Over the sunny roads beyond Santa Maria, where he and Fra Egidio[92] walked singing and exhorting men and women to repentance, we wheeled imploring, or rather commanding, them to get out of the way. It was a hard pull up the mountain-side, the harder because the great monastery on its high foundations seemed always so far above us. When almost at the city gate a monk in brown robes, the knotted cord about his waist, passed. He stopped to look, but it was with a frown of disapproval; I think Saint Francis would have smiled.

Perfect road.

## At Assisi

It was just noon when we reached Assisi, but we rode no more that day. We spent the afternoon in the town of Saint Francis. The *albergo* we selected from the many recommended was without the large cloisters of the monastery. The *cameriere* at once remembered that J— had been there before, though eighteen months had passed since his first visit. The *Signore* had two other ladies with him then, he said. He was delighted with the *velocipede*. It was the first time in all his life he had seen one with three wheels. Nothing would do but he must show us the finest road to Rome. He spread our map on the table, as we eat our dinner, and put on his glasses for he was a little bad in the eyes, he explained, and then he pointed out the very route we had already decided upon. *Ecco!* here between Spoleto and Terni, we should have a long climb up the mountain, but then there would be seven miles down the other side. Ah! that would be fine! This long coast to Terni was clearly to make up for the hardships we had already endured on toilsome up-grades.

After dinner we went to the church. Goethe, when he was in Assisi, saw the old Roman Temple of Minerva, and then, that his pleasure in it might not be disturbed, refused to look at anything else in the town and went quickly on his way. But when I passed out of the sunlight into the dark lower church and under the low, rounded arches to the altar with Giotto's angels and saints above,[93] it seemed to me he was the loser by his great love for classic beauty. Many who have been to this wonderful church have written descriptions of it, but none have really told, and indeed no one can ever tell, how wonderful it is. The upper church, with its great lofty nave and many windows through which the light streams in on the bright frescoed walls, is beautiful. But this lower one, with its dark subdued colour and its dim light and the odour of incense which always lingers in it, is like the embodiment of the mystery and love that inspired the saint in whose honour it was built. In it one understands, for the first time perhaps, what it is for which the followers of St. Francis give up life and action. Whoever were to be long under the influence of this place must, I thought, always stay, like an old grey-haired monk, kneeling before a side altar, rapt in contemplation. And yet on the very threshold I found three or four brothers laughing and joking with two women—Italian Dr. Mary Walkers[94] they must have been, for they wore men's collars and cravats and coats with field glasses slung over their shoulders, and stiff felt hats, and they were smoking long *cigari Cavour*. They were artists and had been painting, Oh so badly! in the church all the morning.

The sun was setting when we left the monastery and walked through the streets, now silent and deserted, where Francis in his gay youth wandered with boon companions, singing not hymns, but love songs. A small boy came and walked with us, and unbidden acted as our guide. Here was the *Duomo*, he said, and here the Church of Santa Chiara; and, when we were on the road without the city gate, *Ecco!* below Santa Maria degli Angeli. For, from where we stood, we looked down upon the huge church rising from the plain, where even now there are scarcely more houses than in the days when Franciscans, coming from far and near to hold counsel with their founder, built their straw huts upon it. Our self-appointed guide was a bright little fellow and never once begged like other children who followed us. So when he showed us the road to Foligno, where we must ride on the morrow, J— gave him a sou. At the door of the albergo he said he must go home, but not to supper; he never had any. He asked at what time we should leave in the morning, when he would like to come and say good-bye. "*Felice notte*"—a happy night—were his last words as he turned away.

## Virgil's Country

The next morning, with a select company of ragged boys, our young guide arrived in time to see us start. When I came out he nodded in a friendly way, as if to an old acquaintance, to the wonder and admiration of the other youngsters. The waiter, his glasses on, came to the gate with us. Two monks, standing there, asked how far we were going on our *velocipede*. "To Rome?" they cried; "why then we are two priests and two pilgrims!" Our guide and his friend ran down the mountain-side after us until we gave the former another sou, when they at once disappeared. It seemed a little ungrateful, but I did not give him much thought, for just then J— bade me back-pedal with all my might. The machine went very fast despite my hard work, and to my surprise J— suddenly steered into a stone pile by the road-side. "The brake is broken," was his explanation as we slowly upset.

Fortunately, however, the upright connecting the band of the brake with the handle had only slipped out of place, and though we could not fix it in again securely, J— could still manage to use it. This, as far as we could see, was the one defect in our tricycle, but defect it was. A nut on the end of the upright would have prevented such an accident. But this is one of the minor particulars in which tricycle-makers—and we have tried many—are careless. We had the rest of the coast without interruption. Half way down our little friend and his followers ran out from under the olives; he had taken a short cut that he might see us again.

From Assisi to Terni was a long day's ride by towns and villages, through fair valleys and over rough mountains. From the foot of the mountain at Assisi, past Monte Subasio, which, bare and rocky, towered above the lower olive-covered hills, the road was level until we rode by Spello with its old Roman gate-way and ruined amphitheatre. But the hill here was not steep, and then again there came a level stretch into Foligno, the first lowland town to which we had come since we left Poggibonsi, and which, with its mass of roofs and lofty dome rising high above the city walls, looked little like the Foligno in Raphael's picture. Already in our short ride, for it is but ten miles from Assisi to Foligno, we noticed a great difference in the people. It was not only that many of the women wore bodices and long ear-rings, and turned their handkerchiefs up on the top of their heads, but they, and the men as well, were less polite and more stupid than the Tuscans or the Umbrians about Perugia. Few spoke to us, and one woman to whom we said good morning was so startled that she thanked us in return, as if unused to such civilities. For all J—'s shouts of a *destra!*—to the right—and *eccomi!* they would not make room for us; and now in Foligno one woman, in her stupidity or obstinacy, walked directly in front of the machine, and when the little wheel caught her dress, through no fault of ours, cried *"Accidente voi!"* the *voi* being a far greater insult than the wishing us an accident. Then she walked on, cursing in loud voice, down the street, by the little stream that runs through the centre of the town and into the market-place, where St. Francis in mistaken obedience to words heard in ecstasy, sold the cloth he had taken from his father that he might have money to re-build the church of San Damiano. Even the beasts we met were as stupid as the people. At our coming horses, donkeys, and oxen tried to run. We therefore looked for at least a light skirmish when, beyond Foligno, a regiment of cavalry in marching order advanced upon us. But the soldiers stood our charge bravely. Only the officer was routed and retreated into the gutter. Then, forgetting military discipline, he turned his back upon his men to see us ride.

We were now on the old Via Flaminia and in the valley of Clitumnus, Virgil's country.[95] The poet's smiling fields and tall, stiff oaks, his white oxen, and peasants behind the plough or enjoying the cool shade, were on either side. Crossing the fields were many stony beds of streams, now dry, lined with oaks and chestnuts, under whose shade women were filling large baskets with acorns and leaves. The upturned earth was rich and brown. Through the trees or over them we saw the whitish-blue sky, the purple mountains, some pointed like pyramids, and the gray olive hills with little villages in their hollows, and before long Trevi on its high hill-top. And then we came to the Temple of the River God, Clitumnus, of which Pliny writes,[96] and where the little river, in which Virgil says the white flocks for the sacrifice bathed, runs below, an old mill on its bank and one willow bending over it.

At the village of Le Vene, near the source of the stream, we stopped at a wine-shop to eat some bread and cheese. There was no one there but the *padrone* and a dwarf who wore a decent suit of black clothes and a medallion of the Pope on his watch-chain. He had come in a carriage which waited for him at the door. I think he was a drummer. He drank much wine, and spoke to us in a vile *patois*. Indeed, the people thereabouts all spoke in dialects worse, I am sure, than any Dante heard at the mouth of Hell.[97] He had travelled and had been in Florence, where he had seen a *velocipede*, but not like ours. It was finer, or perhaps, he should say, more commodious. The seats were side by side, and it had an umbrella attached, and it was worked by the hands. It went, oh, so fast! and he intimated that we could not hope to rival its speed.

*Gathering Leaves.*

I suppose our machine without an umbrella seemed to him like a ship without a sail. But I think he had another tale to tell when, ten minutes later, he having started before we did, we passed him on the road. We were going so fast, I only had time to see that in his wonder the reins fell from his hands.

Then came the small, wretched village of San Giacomo, with its old castle built up with the houses of the poor, and then Spoleto, where we lunched in a *trattoria* of the people, which was much troubled by a plague of flies. A company of *bersaglieri*,[98] red caps on the back of their heads and blue tassels dangling down their backs, sat at one table, ordering with much merriment their soup and meat and macaroni to be cooked a la *bersagliere*. At another two young men were evidently enjoying an unwonted feast. And at the table with us were three peasants, one of whom had brought his bread in his pocket. He ate his soup for dessert, and throughout the meal used his own knife in preference to the knife and fork laid at his place. Two dogs, a cat, and a hen wandered in from the *piazza*, and dined on the bits of macaroni dropped by the not over-careful soldiers. The *cameriere* greeted us cordially. He too had a machine, he said, but had never heard of a *velocipede* with three wheels. His had but two; the Signore must see it. And before he would listen to our order for lunch, he showed J— his bicycle, a bone-shaker.[99] He was very proud of it. He had ridden as far as Terni. Ah! what a beautiful time we should have before the afternoon was over. Seven miles down the mountain!

The thought of this coast made us leave Spoleto with light hearts, though we knew that first must come a hard climb. But if the road was as perfect as it had been all the morning, there was not much to dread. It was half-past two when we started from the *trattoria*, but we were fifteen minutes in walking to the other end of the town. There was no use riding. The streets were narrow and steep and crowded with stupid men and women and donkeys and officers, who instead of controlling were controlled by their horses. Beyond the gate the ascent at first was gradual and we rode easily, even as we worked looking back to the famous old aqueduct and the shadowy heights of Norcia. For some distance we went by the dried-up bed of a wide stream, meeting many priests on foot and peasants on donkeys. But as the way became steeper we left the stream far below, and came into a desolate country where the mountains were covered with scrub oaks, and priests and peasants disappeared. Only one old man kept before us, making short cuts up the mountain side, but after a while he too rode out of sight. We soon gave up riding. J— tied a rope to the tricycle and pulled while I pushed. The sun was now hidden behind the mountain and the way was shady. But still it was warm work and wearisome; for before long the road became almost perpendicular and was full of loose stones. How much more of this was there? we asked a woman watching swine on the hill-side. "A mile," was her answer, and yet she must have known there were at least three. Finally, after what seemed hours of toiling, we asked another peasant standing in front of a lonely farm-house how much farther it still was to the top. "You are here now," she said. She at least was truthful. A few feet more and we looked down a road as precipitous as that up which we had come, and so winding that we could see short stretches of it, like so many terraces, all the way down the mountain. We walked for about a hundred yards, and it was as hard to hold back the machine as before it had been to push it. Then we began to ride, but the strain on the brake loosened the handle a second time. We dismounted, and J— tried to push it back into place. It snapped in two pieces in his hands. Here we were, eight miles from Terni in a lonely mountain road in the evening—the sun had already set—with a brakeless machine which, if allowed to start down hill with its heavy load of two riders and much luggage, would soon be more unmanageable than a run-away horse. The seven miles coast to which we had looked forward for days was to be a walk after all. Like the King of France and his twenty thousand men, we had marched up the mountain that we might march down again. Is it any wonder that we both lost our tempers, and that an accident was the smallest evil we wished the manufacturers of our tricycle? Because they cared more for lightness than for strength, since record-making is as yet the chief end of cycling,[100] the necks of people who ride for pleasure are forsooth to be risked with impunity!

However there was nothing to do but to walk into Terni. It was very cold, and we had to put on our heavy coats. Presently the moon rose above the mountains on our left. By its light we could see the white road, now provokingly good, but steep and winding and all unknown, the hills that shut us in on every side, and, far below, the stream making its way through the narrow pass. The way was unpleasantly lonely and silent; now for an hour or more we went wearily on without hearing a sound but our steady tramp; and now we passed a farm-house within which many voices were raised in anger, while from the barn a dog barked savagely upon our coming. At times we thought we saw in the distance a castle with tall towers or an old ruin, but when we drew near we found in its place great rocks and cliffs of tufa.[101] Once we went through a small village. The way here was not so steep, and for a few minutes we rode. Just beyond the houses three men, driving home a large white bull, walked in the middle of the road. J— shouted that they might give us more space to pass. But they only laughed and tried to set the bull on us with loud cries of *Via!* Before the last died away we were walking again.

On and on we walked, all the time holding back the tricycle. But at last we began to meet more people. Men with carts and donkeys went by at long intervals, but they spake never a word, and we too were silent. Now and then we heard the near tinkling of cow-bells, and came to olive gardens, where in the moonlight the black, twisted trunks took grotesque goblin shapes, and the branches threw a network of shadows across our path. Then we came to a railroad, and we knew we were at the foot of the mountains, and that Terni was not far off. We were at the end of the seven miles' coast and could ride again. Two men just then coming our way, J— asked them how far we were from the town. But they stood still and stared for answer. A second time he asked, and still they were speechless, and we left them there, dumb and motionless. Not far beyond the road divided, and on either side were a few houses. A woman, or a fiend in female form, sat in front of one. "Which is the way to Terni?" we asked. She was silent. Once more we asked. "*Chi lo sa?*"—who knows?—she answered. This was more than tired human nature could endure. J— turned upon her with an arrangement in popular Italian, that conquered her as the prayers of St. Anthony vanquished her sister demons. She arose and meekly showed us the way. In another minute the lights of Terni were in sight. Then we wheeled by a foundry with great furnace in full blast, up a broad avenue with rows of gas-jets, to the gates of the city, to find them shut. There was a second of despair, but J— was now not to be trifled with, and he gave a yell of command which was an effectual "Open, Sesame." And so we rode on through lively streets and piazza to the hotel, to supper and to bed.

## Terni and Its Falls

We know little of Terni, except that the hotel is so cold that the *cameriere* comes into the dining-room in the morning with hat on and wrapped in overcoat and muffler, and that there is an excellent blacksmith in the town, for the next morning, as soon as J— had had the brake mended, he paid the bill and brought out the tricycle. The *padrone* was surprised at the shortness of our stay. Did we not know there were waterfalls, and famous ones too, but three miles distant? We could not take the time to visit them? Well, then, at least we must look at their picture, and he showed us a chromo pasted on the hotel omnibus. I am afraid he took us for sad Philistines. But the fear of another kind of waterfall was still a goad to hurry us onwards. Now we were so near our journey's end, no wonder, however great, could have led us from the straight path.

## In the Lands of Brigands

There was a great *festa* that day, and all along the street and out on the country road we met men and women in holiday dress, carrying baskets and bunches and wreaths of pink chrysanthemums. In Narni, on the heights which Martial called inaccessible, men were lounging in the *piazza* or playing cards in the *caffe*. For the shepherds alone there was no rest from every-day work. Before we reached even Narni, but ten miles across the valley from Terni, we saw several driving their sheep and goats into the broad meadows. They wore goat-skin breeches, and by that sign alone we should have known we were nearing Rome. We lunched at Narni on coffee and cakes, for it was the last town through which we should pass on that day's ride. It was here Quintus, in its Roman prosperity, stayed so long that Martial reproached him for his wearisome delay.[102] Could he come to it now, I doubt if his friend would have the same reason for complaint. It did not seem an attractive place, and when we asked a man about the country beyond, he said it was *"bruto."* We did not learn till afterwards that this applied to the people, and not to the country, and that here we ought to have been briganded.

We were now high up on the mountain, on one side steep rocks, on the other a deep precipice. Far below in a narrow valley ran the little river Nar, and on the bank above it the railroad. It was not an easy road to travel, and often the hills were too steep to coast or to climb. The few farm-houses by the way were closed, for the peasants had gone to church. We saw an occasional little grey town crowning the top of sheer grey cliffs, like those in Albert Dürer's pictures,[103] or an old castle either deserted or else with farm-house built in its ruins, where peasants leaned over the battlemented walls. But the only villages through which we rode were Otricoli, just before we descended to the valley of the Tiber, where we created so great a sensation that an old woman selling chestnuts, cooked, I think, by a previous generation, was at first too frightened to wait on us; and Borghetto, on the other side of the valley, where we saw in the *piazza* the stage from Civita Castellana, in which town we were to spend the night.

There were a few people abroad. In the loneliest part of the mountain an old man in a donkey-cart kept in front of us on a long up-grade. Interested in the tricycle, he forgot the donkey, which gave up a straight for a spiral course, and monopolised the road. J— angrily asked its driver which side he meant to take. But the old man heaped coals of fire on his head by offering to carry us up in his waggon. After we left him far behind we passed two travellers resting by the wayside. Their bags lay on the ground, and they looked weary and worn. They gave us good day, and where were we going, they of course wanted to know. They too were bound for Rome, it turned out, and had come from Bologna. After the two gentlemen of Bologna we overtook a group of merry peasants, coats slung over their shoulders for no possible reason but for the sake of picturesqueness, and hats adorned with gay pompons of coloured paper and tinsel. One carried branches of green leaves and red fruit like cherries, and as we went by he gave us a branch and wished us a good journey. Next went by an old woman who said with a smile that we could go without horse or donkey—a witticism heard so often it could no longer make us laugh. And then a little boy, all alone, came piping down the valleys wild.

We went with much content over the plain by the Tiber, where there were broad grassy stretches full of sheep and horses, and here and there the shepherds' gipsy-looking huts. It was such easy work now that we ate our chestnuts as we rode; but beyond the bridge, on which Sixtus V. and Clement VIII. and

Gregory XIII. have, in true papal fashion, left their names, the hills began again. On we toiled, beneath shady oaks and by rocky places, until we came out on a wide upland. From the treeless road the meadows rolled far beyond to high mountains on whose sloping side the blue smoke of charcoal-burners curled upward. The moon had already risen, and in the west the setting sun filled the sky with glowing amber light, against which the tired peasants going home were sharply silhouetted.

We were glad to see Civita Castellana. One or two men in answer to our questions had told us we were close to it, but we did not believe them. The fields seemed to stretch for miles before us, and there was not a house or tower in sight. But suddenly the road turned and went down-hill, and there below was the city perched on tufa cliffs, a deep ravine surrounding it. Two *carabinieri*, in cocked hats and folded cloaks like the famous two solitary horsemen, were setting out on their night patrol. Vespers were just over in the church near the bridge, and along the way where happy little Etruscan school-boys once whipped homewards their treacherous schoolmaster, little Italian boys and girls let loose from church ran after us, torturing us with their shrill cries. Soon their elders joined them, and we were closely beset with admirers. The town, too, was in a hubbub about us, and in the streets through which we wheeled men and women came from their houses to follow in our train. At the door of the *albergo*, where we were detained for several minutes, the entire population collected. We had difficulty in getting a room. The *festa*, the *padrone* said, had brought many country people into the town, and the inns were full to overflowing. If J— would go with him he would see what could be done for us. The search led them through three houses. In the meantime I kept guard over the machine. It was well I did, for when J— had gone the natives closed upon me. Toddling infants and grey-haired men, ragged peasants and gorgeous officers pushed and struggled together in their desire to see. Every now and then a stealthy hand was thrust through the crowd and felt the tyre or tried the brake. I turned from left to right, crying *Guarda! Guarda!* I lifted exploring hands from the wheels. But in vain. What was one against so many? A man sitting in the doorway took pity on my sad plight. He came out and with a stick mowed the people back. Then J— returned, having found a room in the first house, which the *padrone* had thought fit to conceal until the last.

## A Middling Inn

The *albergo* of Civita Castellana was but a "middling inn." The *padrone*, in English tweed, high boots and Derby hat, looked half cockney, half brigand. His wife wore an elaborate false front and much lace about her neck. But they were far finer than their house. We were lodged in the garret, in a room the size of a large closet. The way to it led through another bed-chamber, long and low, in which four cots were ranged in a row along the wall. When we crossed it on the way down stairs to dinner, I devoutly prayed that on our return four night-caps would not be nodding on the pillows. Later in the evening when we had dined we strolled out to the *piazza*. To see the life of an Italian town you have only to go to the *caffe*. We went to one near the *albergo*. There were two tables in it. We sat at the smaller, and at the other were four ragged boys playing cards.

Fortunately we were the first to go to bed in the garret. All through the night, however, for the mattress was hard and I slept little, I heard loud snores and groans, and the sound of much tossing to and fro. We rose early in the morning, but when we opened our door the cots were empty, though they had not been so long.


## Across the Roman Campagna

Early as we were, the whole town was stirring when we came down stairs. But who ever knew the hour when the people of an Italian town were not up and abroad? No sooner did J— bring the tricycle from the stable, where it had been kept all night, to the *albergo*, than the *piazza* was again crowded. On they all came with us, men, women, and children, hooting and shouting, jumping and dancing through the vilely paved streets and finally sprawling over the walls and on to the rocks beyond the gate.

There they all stayed until we had gone down the hill, over the bridge crossing the stream at its foot, and up the hill on its opposite side, passing from their sight round the first curve. Soon we were on an upland, and now really at the beginning of the Campagna. The morning was cold. For many miles we rode through a champaign gleaming white with frost. But as the sun rose higher in the heavens, and the yellow light, which had at first spread over the sky, faded and left a clear blue expanse above, the air grew warmer and the frost disappeared. The road wound on and on between oak woods and wide, cultivated fields, and green grassy plains which gradually changed into great

*From Via Flaminia, near Ponte Molle.*

sweeps of rolling, treeless country, like the moors. By the roadside were thick bushes of low green sage and tangled blackberries, and in places the broad flagstones of the old Flaminian Way, with weeds and dandelions and pretty purple flowers growing from the crevices. Sometimes a paving of smaller stones stretched all across the road, so that for a minute or two we were badly shaken, or else, coming on them suddenly at the foot of a hill, all but upset. Truly, as has been said, it could have been no joke for the old Romans to ride. To our left rose the great height of Soracte, not snow-covered as Horace saw it, but bare and brown save where purple shadows lay.[104] At first we met numbers of peasants, all astride of donkeys, going towards Civita Castellana, families riding together and eating as they went. Later, however, no one passed but an occasional lonely rider, who in his long cloak and high-pointed hat looked a genuine Fra Diavolo;[105] or else sportsmen and their dogs. It is strange that though we saw many of the latter, we never once heard the singing or chirping of birds. There were hill-sides and fields full of large black cattle, or herds of horses, or flocks of sheep and goats. There were shepherds, too, sleeping in the shade, or by the roadside leaning on their staffs or ruling their flocks with rod and rustic word as in the days when Poliziano sang.[106] And if there was no bird's song to break the silence of the Campagna, there was instead a loud baaing of sheep, led by the shrill, piercing notes of the lambs. If it was to such an accompaniment that Corydon and Thyrsis sang in rivalry, their songs could have been poetical only in Virgil's verse.[107]

How hard we worked now that our pilgrimage was almost ended! We scarcely looked at the little village through which we wheeled, and where a White Brother was going from door to door, nor at the ruins which rose here and there in the hollows and on the slopes of the hills; and when at last we saw on the horizon the dome coming up out of the broad, undulating plain, we gave it but a short greeting and then hurried on faster than ever. We would not even go to Castel Nuovo, which lies a quarter of a mile or so from the road, but ate our hasty lunch in a *trattoria* by the wayside, while a man, an engineer he said he was, showed us drawings he had made on his travels, and asked about our ride. How brave it was of the *Signora* to work, he exclaimed, and how brave of the *Signore* to sketch from his *velocipede!* And after this "the hills their heights began to lower," and with feet up we went like the wind, and every time we looked at the dome it seemed larger and more clearly defined against the sky. But about six miles from Rome our feet were on the pedals again and we were working with all our might. Sand and loose stones covered the road, which grew worse until, in front of the staring pink quarantine building, the stones were so many that in steering out of the way of one we ran over another, and the jar it gave us loosened the screw of the luggage-carrier. We were so near Rome we let it go. This was a mistake. But a little farther, and the whole thing gave way and bags and knapsack rolled in the dust. It took some fifteen minutes to set it to rights again; and all the time we stood in the shadeless road, under a burning sun, for the heat in the lower plains of the Campagna was as great as if it were still summer. As the luggage-carrier was slightly broken, we were afraid to put too great a strain upon it, and for the rest of the journey the knapsack went like a small boy swinging on behind.

Like those other pilgrims, we were much discouraged because of the way. But at last, wheeling by pink and white *trattorie*, whose walls were covered with illustrated bills of fare, and coming to an open place where street-cars

*Stop!*

were going and coming, the Ponte Molle, over a now yellow Tiber, lay before us, and we were under the shadow of the dome we had from afar watched for many hours. Over the bridge we went with cars and carts, between houses and gardens and wine-shops, where there was a discord of many hurdy-gurdies, to the Porta del Popolo, and so into Rome. *Carabinieri* were lounging about the gate, and carriages were driving to the Pincian; but we rode on and up the street on the right of the *piazza*. When we had gone a short distance we asked a man at a corner our way to the Piazza di Spagna. We should have taken the street to our left, he said, but now we could reach it by crossing the Corso diagonally. As we did so we heard a loud *sst, sst* behind us, and we saw a *gendarme* running up the street; but we went on. When we wheeled into the Piazza di Spagna, however, a second, almost breathless, ran out in front of us, and cried, "Stop!" But still we rode. "Stop!" he cried again, and half drew his sword. In a minute we were surrounded. Models came flying from the Spanish steps; an old countryman carrying a fish affectionately under his arm, boot-blacks, clerks from the near shops, young Roman swells—all these and many more gathered about us.

"Stop!" the *gendarme* still cried.

"Why?" we asked.

And then his fellow-officer, whom we had seen on the Corso came up. "Get down!" he said in fierce tones of command.

"Why?" we asked again.

"*Per Christo!*"[108] was his only answer.

The crowd laughed with glee. Hackmen shouted their applause. It was ignominious, perhaps, but the wisest policy to get down and walk to our hotel.

## The Finish

What pilgrim of old times thought his pilgrimage really over until he had given either out of his plenty or his nothing, in alms? Two months later we too gave our mite, not to the Church or to the poor, but to the Government; for we were then summoned before a police magistrate and fined ten francs for "*furious* riding on the Corso, and refusing to descend when ordered!"[109]

And so our pilgrimage ended.

# Notes

## INTRODUCTION

1. The article actually appeared in *The Century Illustrated Monthly Magazine* in two parts: "Italy from a Tricycle" 31.5 (Mar. 1886): 644–64, and "Italy, from a Tricycle" 31.6 (Apr. 1886): 839–59.
2. Hereafter referenced as *LL1* and *LL2*.
3. See sections titled "The Pennells' Cycling Publications" and "Non-Cycling Books by the Pennells" in this volume's bibliography.
4. For instance, Howells's *Tuscan Cities* (1885) and *Italian Journeys* (1895); James's *A Little Tour in France* (1900) and *Italian Hours* (1909); Irving's *The Alhambra* (1896).
5. The Pennells rather shrewdly made the most of their connections to Whistler, producing several books about him and his work, including *The Whistler Journal* (1921) and *Whistler, the Friend* (1930).
6. *Life of Mary Wollstonecraft* (1884), *Charles Godfrey Leland: A Life* (1906), *Life and Letters of Joseph Pennell* (1929).
7. Originally published as *The Feasts of Autolycus: The Diary of a Greedy Woman*. London: J. Lane, 1896.
8. See Leonard N. Beck, *Two Loaf Givers; or, a Tour through the Gastronomic Libraries of Katherine Golden Bitting and Elizabeth Robins Pennell*. Washington, DC: Library of Congress, 1984.
9. See Talia Schaffer, *The Forgotten Female Aesthetes: Literary Culture in Late-Victorian England*. Charlottesville: UP of Virginia, 2000; Meaghan Clarke, *Critical Voices: Women and Art Criticism in Britain, 1880–1905* (London: Ashgate, 2005); Jane S. Gabin, *American Women in Gilded Age London: Expatriates Rediscovered* (Gainesville: U of Florida P, 2006). Kimberly Morse Jones, "A Bibliography of the New Art Criticism of Elizabeth Robins Pennell," *Victorian Periodicals Review* 41.3 (Fall 2008): 270–87, and "'Making a Name for Whistler': Elizabeth Robins Pennell as a New Art Critic" in *Women in Journalism at the Fin de Siècle: Making a Name for Herself*, ed. F. Elizabeth Gray (London: Palgrave Macmillan, 2012): 129–45. On Pennell's food writing, see Jamie Horrocks, "Camping in the Kitchen: Locating Culinary Authority in Elizabeth Robins Pennell's *Delights of Delicate Eating*." *Nineteenth-Century Gender Studies* 3.2 (Summer 2007); Talia Schaffer, "The Importance

of Being Greedy: Connoisseurship and Domesticity in the Writings of Elizabeth Robins Pennell." *The Recipe Reader: Narratives, Contexts, Traditions*, Eds. Janet Floyd and Laurel Forster (Burlington, VT: Ashgate, 2003): 105–26.

10. Published in the United States as *Two Pilgrims' Progress: From Fair Florence, to the Eternal City of Rome* (Boston: Roberts Brothers, 1886/87).

11. Early safety bicycles, such as the popular Rover, featured a slightly larger front wheel, but by the boom of the 1890s, front and back wheels tended to be the same size.

12. Reade published *Nauticus on his Hobby-Horse: Or the Adventures of a Sailor During a Tricycle Cruise of 1427 Miles* (1880) and a sequel, *Nauticus in Scotland: A Tricycle Tour of 2462 Miles* (1882). Kron produced some of the earliest American cycling journalism in the pages of *The Wheelman* and other magazines and later in his massive "cyclopedia" of cycling lore, *Ten Thousand Miles on a Bicycle* (1887).

13. Lenz wrote about his adventures in a series of dispatches that appeared in *Outing* between 1892 and 1897, entitled "Around the World with Wheel and Camera." He disappeared in Asia and Sachtleben and Allen set off to follow his route and discover what happened to Lenz. Their account is called *Across Asia on a Bicycle* (1894). For more on Lenz, as well as Sachtleben and Allen, see David V. Herlihy's *The Lost Cyclist* (New York: Houghton Mifflin, 2010).

14. Although this article appeared unsigned in *The Century* in September 1884, we know that it was written by Elizabeth (*LL1*: 106).

15. I consider the term *tricycle* to include certain four-wheeled cycles from this period. The fourth wheel was usually a small guide wheel or "tipping wheel" at the front of the machine.

16. Glen Norcliffe refers to this period as the little-recognized "tricycle boom." See his "On the Technical and Social Significance of the Tricycle." *Cycle History 17: Proceedings of the Seventeenth International Cycle History Conference*, Ed. Glen Norcliffe (San Francisco: Van der Plas, 2007) 59–68.

17. See Twain's *What Is Man? And Other Essays* (New York: Harper & Brothers, 1917).

18. Norcliffe points out that, despite the common perception of tricycles as slow, tricycle racing was popular in the early 1880s and that two riders on a racing tandem tricycle could hold their own with many highwheelers. Newspapers of the period occasionally mention tricycle-bicycle races.

19. The social aspect was key to the rise of the tricycle. In the early 1880s, it became fashionable in cities such as London, Dublin, and Boston for gentlefolk to be seen out tricycling on their "sociables," as side-by-side tandems came to be known. Tricycle clubs and magazines sprang up in these cities, and while the high-wheelers were often obsessed with speed, many tricyclists had other priorities. American and British outdoor and popular periodicals of the day featured articles about tricycling and handbooks began to appear advising what machines to buy, what clothes to wear while riding and what places to travel to.

20. See also George B. Thayer's *Pedal and Path: Across the Continent Awheel and Afoot* (Hartford: Evening Post Association, 1887), and Hugh Callan's *Wanderings on Wheel and on Foot through Europe* (London: Sampson Low, Marston, Searle, & Rivington, 1887).

21. The rise of tricycles was, for some, a class phenomenon. Dodge argues that "the tricycle developed quickly into an aristocratic form of cycling, to be distinguished from the 'lower classes' of bicycles. Tricycles were dignified, and tricycles [were] expensive" (76), a fact that meant the working classes were excluded from the tricycle ranks. Queen Victoria's decision to order two Salvo sociable tricycles in 1881 helped further the aristocratic associations of tricycle riding. However, the Pennells were far from aristocrats, and their cycling ethos emphasized the liberating, egalitarian appeal of tricycling: it was something everyone could do.

22. Kron lists an L.H. Johnson and his wife; H.C. Douglas and his wife; L.H. Porter and his wife. He says he could cite more examples but to do so would "make the bachelor compiler [Kron's term for himself] sad at heart," so he stops (530).

23. American Dan Canary was a pioneer bicycle trick rider, well known in the 1880s for his daring and imaginative performances at six-day races, circuses, and show halls from London to Paris to New York. See the profile of Canary in *Argosy* 7.18 (1889): 588.

24. In Elizabeth's London diary, she tells of Joseph going to a tricycle meet on 9 May 1886 in London and seeing Thomas Stevens "with his nickel-plated machine."

25. In 1887, Karl Kron listed twenty-two different cycling publications that he knew to be active in the United States, England, Canada, Ireland, and Australia in 1886 (655). He also listed numerous other cycling periodicals that had been active earlier in the 1880s but were no longer operational.

26. See, for instance, J.G. Dalton (ed.), *Lyra Bicyclical: Forty Poets on the Wheel* (1880), and Foster S. Conant's *Wheel Songs: Poems of Bicycling* (1884). As for cycling novels, one of the first was Florine Thayer Maccray and Esther Louise Smith's *Wheels and Whims: An Etching* (1884), about four women who take a three-week tricycle excursion (with a chaperone) along the Connecticut River. Perhaps the best-known early cycling novel is H.G. Wells's *The Wheels of Chance: A Bicycling Idyll* (1896) about a draper's assistant who takes a cycling summer holiday during which he meets and rescues a young lady.

27. Hereafter referenced as *OP*.

28. Leland had been a successful journalist in Philadelphia and then made a splash with *The Breitmann Ballads* and a series of gypsy books including *The English Gipsies* [sic] *and their Language* (1873) and *The Gypsies* (1882).

29. Her first commission from the *Evening Telegraph* did not lead to further work with that paper. In her memoir, *Our Philadelphia*, Elizabeth writes that although she was proud of this piece, "I am afraid it left the Editor indifferent" (246). However, *The Atlantic Monthly* published eight pieces by Robins between 1881 and 1883.

30. Chapter title in Elizabeth's memoir *Our Philadelphia* (268).

31. However, there are some exceptions. In their biography of Whistler, for instance, Elizabeth's name comes first, and they employ a third-person "we." In one of their non-cycling travel books from 1892, *Play in Provence*, they alternate chapters—one in his voice, the next in hers, and so on. See the section titled "The Pennells' Cycling Publications" in this volume's bibliography.

32. Their first published cycle-travel collaboration was a magazine piece for *The Century* about Joseph's tricycle ride from Coventry to Chester in 1883. The editors wanted

Joseph's illustrations, but they rejected his original accompanying story. So he asked Elizabeth to rewrite it for him, supposedly in his voice (never mind that she had never been to England at that point), and the revised version appeared in September of 1884, unsigned (*LL1*: 106).

33. Hereafter referred to as P-WC.

34. Several of Elizabeth's letters to Joseph make reference to this practice of her writing "cycling notes" she considers to be Joseph's. For instance, in a letter to Joseph dated 8 April 1891, she mentions "writing your C.Y.C. Notes for the *Pall Mall*" (P-WC, box 305). And elsewhere in letters she refers to having written "my cycling notes" as well as "columns" for both *The Pall Mall Gazette* and *The Penny Illustrated Paper* (P-WC, box 307).

35. Pennell's illustrations from that trip appeared in Howells's *Tuscan Cities* (1886).

36. The term *Convertible* is used by the Pennells, and found often in tricycling literature of the day. It probably refers to options of removing wheels to make storage easier or switching the seats on a tandem from front and back to side by side (the "sociable" arrangement, as it was known). See Norcliffe's "The Coventry Tricycle: Technology, Gender, and Buzz." *Cycle History 19: Proceedings of the Nineteenth International Cycle History Conference*, 2008, Ed. Anne Henry (St. Etienne: Musée d'Arts et d'Industries, 2010): 136–43.

37. For their second trip, to Italy, the Pennells switched to a Humber Tandem Tricycle. The illustration on the cover and title page of *A Canterbury Pilgrimage* shows the Pennells on the Humber, even though they did not use it on that ride.

38. See, for instance, William Howitt's *Homes and Haunts of the Most Eminent British Poets*, 2 vols. (1847). The Pennells seem to have inspired a subgenre of literary cycling pilgrimages, such as F.W. Bockett's *Some Literary Landmarks for Pilgrims on Wheels* (1901) and, perhaps, Charles S. Brooks's *A Thread of English Road* (1924).

39. An extended excerpt from the book appeared in *Outing* 6.6 (Sep. 1885): 725–30.

40. In February 1887, the Pennells were delighted to learn that *Outing* magazine had included *A Canterbury Pilgrimage* in its "Wheeling" section of their list of the 100 best books about sport ever published (479). This section included two other cycle-touring books, A.D. Chandler and J.C. Sharp's *A Bicycle Tour in England and Wales* (1881) and *Nauticus on his Hobby-Horse* (1880) by "Nauticus," the pseudonym for tricyclist Charles Edward Reade, who also wrote a sequel, *Nauticus in Scotland* (1882).

41. An unidentified newspaper clipping tucked in Elizabeth's 1885 diary states that the book was in "its 12th thousand in London."

42. Elizabeth's diary mentions that Joseph was called upon at a Society of Cyclists meeting to "say a few words and introduced as 'The Canterbury Pilgrim'" [as if there were only one] (27 Oct. 1885). At a Pickwick Society meeting, "everybody cried for Joe, Joe Pennell, and he had to make a speech" (5 Dec. 1885).

43. The two books by "Nauticus" and the one by Chandler and Sharp are the only English-language cycle-touring books I know of published before *A Canterbury Pilgrimage*.

44. At this time, many *leisure* cyclists drew attention to this distinction between what Karl Kron, in 1887, called the "[q]uiet tourists" on cycles and the "showy racers." Kron argued that "racers are nothing more than the foam and froth on the surface of Niagara's whirlpool; they are pretty to look at and convenient to chat about; yet, as the real power

and mystery of the pool lie hidden in the depths, so the true spirit and permanent charm of cycling are best exemplified by the army of quiet riders who never display themselves upon a race-track" (v).

45. The term *picturesque* goes back to at least the mid-eighteenth century, and the context of landscape painting. *Picturesque* referred to a somewhat formulaic and artificial style of landscape painting which meant to evoke images from Roman pastoral poetry (from the first century AD) and to recall the work of seventeenth-century French painters such as Claude Lorrain and Salvator Rosa. In the 1790s the term took on a slightly broader meaning as it also came to be applied to gardening and travel writing too, and began to refer to landscapes that emphasized irregularity, dishevelment, and decay—features that, according to proponents of the picturesque, such as William Gilpin, allowed artists a certain variety and boldness of touch.

    The 1790s was the heyday of the picturesque in England: that decade saw a proliferation of picturesque landscape art and travel narratives to classic picturesque locations such as the Lake Country and Wales. But the picturesque aesthetic lived on in the nineteenth century, especially in the United States, though in a more populist aesthetic. By the 1860s and 1870s, the term *picturesque* had become so widely used in travel writing as to become a cliché. In common parlance, picturesque conveyed simply the sense of a pleasing image of an idealized, usually rural, beauty that is often associated with, well, *pictures* and paintings, in general. In visual art, according to Louis Hawes, the picturesque emphasized "variety and contrast of color, light and shade, sudden variation of shape, rough texture, and, above all, rich and shadowy foreground flanked with assorted trees or rambling irregular shrubbery infusing a certain cosy or quaint look and feeling" (*Presences of Nature: British Landscape, 1780–1830* (New Haven, CT: Yale Center for British Art, 1982): 39). In terms of travel writing, the picturesque style was light and often sentimental, concerned with the quaint and charming in landscapes and human subjects.

46. For more on the Pennells' connection to the picturesque tradition see my "Cycling and the Picturesque: Cycle-Travel Writing of the 1880s," Ed. Anne Henry, *Cycle History 19: Proceedings of the Nineteenth International Cycling History Conference.* (St. Etienne: Musée d'Arts et d'Industries, 2008): 67–72.

47. Elizabeth later explained that "[h]e and Pennell met also at cycling dinners and meetings, for he [Furnivall] was an ardent cyclist, though not popular among wheelmen, that winter damning himself with them by refusing to drink the health of the queen. Why should he?—he was a republican, was his explanation to us" (*LL*1: 156).

48. Elizabeth seems to forget the problems with the brake and the luggage carrier mentioned in *An Italian Pilgrimage.*

49. There is one other very minor literary pilgrimage connection in the book. In the final appendix-like chapter of the English edition, "Vetturino *versus* Tricycle," not included here, Joseph explains that part of their route followed (albeit in reverse) that of compatriot Nathaniel Hawthorne, who travelled between Rome and Florence in 1858 with his family. Joseph presents a curious, short comparison of their journeys, offering extracts from Hawthorne's notebook side-by-side with his own notes of the final five days of

their journey. However, nowhere in the Pennells' book proper is there any other mention of Hawthorne. In fact, Joseph suggests that it wasn't until he arrived in Rome that he became aware of having shared a route with Hawthorne at all.

50. See also "To Rome on a Tricycle" in *The Pall Mall Gazette* (9 Dec. 1886): 10; and a review in *The Standard* (8 Feb. 1887): 2.

51. This reviewer praises a few episodes, such as the parts about Monte Oliveto, the Siena theatre, and the "enthusiastic bicyclist," but overall complains that the tricycle "pervades" the book, and "instead of making the travel-sketch more unique, it seems to get in the way clumsily" ("Light Travel" 701).

52. Nevertheless, the Pennells continued to use the pilgrimage motif: in *Our Journey to the Hebrides* (1889), which follows the route of Samuel Johnson and James Boswell, and in *To Gipsyland* as well, which saw the Pennells travel to Hungary in search of authentic gypsies. In addition, Elizabeth's diaries mention a scheme for a Percy Shelley pilgrimage, and in her biography of her husband, she mentions the possibility of an "American Pilgrimage," neither of which happened, or at least wasn't written about, to my knowledge.

53. Their first book, however, remained popular throughout this period. On 8 March 1890, the Pennells, writing anonymously in their "Cycle and Camera" column in *The Penny Illustrated Paper*, note that the book was being re-issued yet again. They describe it as "one of the first accounts of a cycling tour which seemed to catch on, and apparently is still catching on with the general as well as the cycling public" (154).

54. According to Norcliffe, the "tricycle boom" ended around 1886, precisely when the Pennells' Italian book appeared.

55. They later regretted this decision, finding that foot travel was more tiring and much slower than that awheel, especially with the art supplies they carried. The "rate of progress bored us," she admits (*LL1*: 192–93). The book, *Our Journey to the Hebrides* (1889), received mixed reviews.

56. Elizabeth was interested in stories about strong, independent women. In addition to unsuccessfully pitching a biography of Catherine of Siena for the same Famous Women series that published her Wollstonecraft book, Elizabeth also proposed one about Amelia Opie, but it, too, was rejected by the editor, Ingram, in a letter dated 10 April 1885 (Box 374, Library of Congress).

57. "Cycling." In *Ladies in the Field: Sketches of Sport*, Ed. The Lady [Beatrice Violet] Greville (New York: D. Appleton & Co., 1894): 247–65.

58. "Every woman is free to make herself ridiculous, and it is none of my business if my neighbours choose to make a public spectacle of themselves by struggling in the arms of policemen, or going into hysterics at meetings where nobody wants them; if they like to emulate bad boys by throwing stones and breaking windows, or if it amuses them to slap and whip unfortunate statesmen who, physically could easily convince them of their inferiority. But when they make themselves a nuisance to me personally I draw the line" (*Our House* 330).

59. In her biography of Joseph, Elizabeth claims Joseph forsook cycling altogether in 1903 after he had a nasty tricycle accident and became increasingly interested in motorcycling (*LL2*: 4–5).

60. Cole's book *The Gypsy Road: A Journey from Krakow to Coblentz* (London: T. Fisher Unwin, 1894) traced much of the Pennells' route to Hungary described in *To Gipsyland*. The Workmans wrote several cycle-travel books, including *Algerian Memories: A Bicycle Tour over the Atlas to the Sahara* (New York: Anson D.F. Randolph & Co., 1985). The Willises published books under the names Allan Eric and "The Junior" Partner: *Following the Tow-path and through the Adirondacks Awheel* (1898) and *Montreal by Way of Chazy and Down the St. Laurence River to Quebec* (1899).

61. The Southern Veteran-Cycle Club issued a reprinted edition of *A Canterbury Pilgrimage*, with an attached souvenir programme, to commemorate this centenary ride.

62. http://www.experienceplus.com/blog/?p=246

63. Elizabeth Robins Pennell, "Twenty Years of Cycling" *Fortnightly Review* 68 (62 n.s.), (Aug. 1897), p. 188.

## A CANTERBURY PILGRIMAGE

1. The Pennells were admirers of Stevenson's early travel writing, especially his *Travels with a Donkey in the Cévennes* (1879). In addition to this dedication, there are numerous other references to Stevenson's work in the Pennells' magazine articles and books, including three mentions in their book *A Sentimental Journey through France and Italy* (1887). The Pennells never met R.L. Stevenson, though they did receive a short letter of thanks from him following the appearance of this book. In London, the Pennells were friends with R.L. Stevenson's cousin, the art critic R.A.M. (Bob) Stevenson.

2. The Strand is a short, famous street in the City of Westminster, London, home of Trafalgar Square and Temple Bar. In the late nineteenth century, the Lancaster Pike was a popular cycle-touring road linking Philadelphia with the city of Lancaster, Pennsylvania, a distance of about 67 miles (108 km). See "Cycling. Notes of the Month," *Outing* 32.3 (June 1898): 319–22.

3. The opening sentence echoes the opening twenty or so lines of the General Prologue to Geoffrey Chaucer's *The Canterbury Tales* (*CT*) in which the speaker announces the time of year (spring, in that case), weather conditions, and natural cycles being appropriate for a pilgrimage to Canterbury.

4. The Tabard Inn, mentioned in l.20 of the General Prologue of *CT*, as the starting point "in Southwerk" for Chaucer's pilgrims. All *CT* references from *The Riverside Chaucer*, 3rd ed., Ed. Larry D. Benson (Boston: Houghton Mifflin, 1987).

5. Road surface made of rectangular, cut stones, similar to cobblestones. In the late nineteenth century in England and Europe, most rural roads were made of dirt, but some cities featured sections of Belgian paving. These stretches of road were notoriously loud for horse and carriages, and jarring for cyclists on hard, non-pneumatic tires, like the ones on the Pennells' tricycle.

6. In the Prologue of the Reeve's Tale, the host urges the Reeve to start his story: "Set forth thy tale, and tarie nat the tyme / Lo Depeford, and it is half-way prime!" (*CT* ll.3905–06) meaning it is about 7:30 a.m.

7. A brook or spring approximately two miles from London on the Old Kent Road; the brook is dedicated to St. Thomas à Becket. In the General Prologue, we are told that the pilgrims "pass / Unto the Wateryng of Seint Thomas" (*CT* ll.825–26).

8. In chapter 5 of Dickens's novel *David Copperfield* (1849–1850), the young hero is sent away from home and walks from London to Dover along this road.

9. Prince Arthur, 1st Duke of Connaught and Strathearn (1850–1942), was the third son of Queen Victoria, and attended Royal Military Academy at Woolwich. He went on to become the 10th Governor General of Canada. Princess Sophia (1777–1848) was the twelfth child of King George III and Charlotte.

10. Deep, wooded valleys or dells (*OED*).

11. In Greek myth, Daphnis, the human son of Hermes and a nymph, was said to have invented pastoral poetry.

12. Pierre-Jean de Béranger (1780–1857) was a French poet and *chansonnier* of the Romantic period. His popular music, such as "Le Vieux Vagabond," depicted romanticized Bohemian figures.

13. The Gardens are mentioned by Charles Dickens, Jr., son of the novelist, in his *Dictionary of the Thames*: "These popular and well-conducted gardens are on the high road to the west of Gravesend, and can be reached direct from the steamboat-pier. The admission is 6d., and there is a constant succession of amusement throughout the day; dancing on the circular platform from 2 o'clock to 11 being a special and favourite feature. Besides the tea and shrimps so dear to the heart of the Gravesend excursionist, other refreshments of a more substantial and stimulating character can be obtained at very reasonable rates. The extent of the grounds, which are tastefully laid out and produce abundance of flowers, is about 20 acres. There is a conservatory about 200 feet long, a bijou theatre, a maze, museum, 'baronial hall,' occasionally used for dancing, but more often for purposes of refreshment. There is a very good fernery and a bear-pit, and some two miles of walks are held out as additional inducements to the excursion public. The peculiar situation of Rosherville—it being an old chalk quarry—has lent itself admirably to the landscape gardener's art, and the result is a really pretty and remarkably diversified garden, in which it is quite feasible to pass that 'Happy Day' which in the advertisements is always coupled with the name of Rosherville" (218).

14. In the introduction to the Pardoner's Tale, just before the Prologue, the host says "here at this alestake / I wol bothe drynke and eten of a cake" (*CT* lines 321–22). An *alestake* is a pole hung with a garland, indicating an alehouse. *Cake* refers to a loaf of bread.

15. Peninsular and Oriental Steam Navigation Company, headquartered in London in the late nineteenth century.

16. In Act 2, scene 2 of Shakespeare's *Henry IV, Part 1*, Gad's Hill is the scene of a highway robbery of some Canterbury pilgrims, perpetrated by Falstaff and his rascally associates, and where Harry plays a practical joke on Falstaff—hiding his horse.

17. Dickens bought a house at Gad's Hill, just outside Rochester, in 1856 and eventually took up permanent residence there until his death in 1870. He had first seen the handsome country house as a child and dreamed of one day living there. According to Dickens, his father often told him, "'If you were to be very persevering and were to work hard, you might some day come to live in it'" (qtd. in Slater 8).

18. Cyclists' Touring Club, an organization headquartered in London and devoted to promoting cycle touring. By the mid-1880s, it "had established chapters around the world and its membership surged past the ten thousand mark" (Herlihy 221).

19. Dickens published an essay "Dullborough Town" in the periodical *All the Year Round* (30 June 1860). (Elizabeth omits an "l" in her spelling.) His fictional Dullborough is a composite of three actual towns: Chatham, Strood, and Rochester. The tone of this essay is a combination of nostalgia and satire (Slater 6).

20. Protaganist John Jasper, music teacher, choirmaster, and soloist—and opium addict—in Dickens's final (unfinished) novel, *The Mystery of Edwin Drood* (1870).

21. The guardian of Rosa Bud, Drood's fiancée and student of John Jasper in *The Mystery of Edwin Drood*.

22. In Jonathan Swift's *Gulliver's Travels* (1726), the Lilliputians (Pennell's spelling is short an l) are a race of tiny humans Gulliver meets on his first voyage, while the Brobdingnagians (and here her spelling is short an n) are a race of giants Gulliver encounters on his second.

23. The Bull Inn (later the Royal Victoria and Bull Hotel), High Street, Rochester, figures in Dickens's *Posthumous Papers of the Pickwick Club* (1836–1837). The Inn was visited by the fictional Mr. Pickwick and associates, who remarked on its "nice beds" (Chapter 2). The Inn later became a regular stop on tours of Dickens's territory. See, for instance, *A Week's Tramp in Dickens' Land* by W.R. Hughes (London: Chapman and Hall, 1891).

24. A British lobbying body devoted to cycling advocacy and safety as well as regulation of cycle racing. It began as the Bicycle Union in 1878, and was joined with the Tricycle Association in 1882 to form the National Cyclists' Union. Among its many initiatives were legal campaigns fighting for protection of cyclists "from hostile coachmen and overzealous policemen" (Herlihy 221).

25. Virgil's "Eclogue 5" is a dialogue between these two rival characters who engage in a kind of singing contest.

26. A good way to go!

27. In *Culture and Anarchy: An Essay in Political and Social Criticism* (1869), Arnold deplores the empty-headed smugness and Philistinism of middle-class Victorian England and encourages a campaign to educate the masses, so they will strive to move beyond "faith in machinery" (89) and toward increased spiritual activity—what he calls "sweetness and light" (50).

28. This probably means working against the pedals to slow the machine on a downhill.

29. Boughton under Blen (or Blean) is a road between Faversham and Canterbury mentioned in the Canon Yeoman's Prologue (*CT* line 556).

30. Lines 556–58 of the Canon Yeoman's Prologue of *The Canterbury Tales*. "Atake" means overtake.

31. Opening lines of the Manciple's Prologue. *Wete* means know. The *blee* is the Blen forest.

32. Erasmus was a Dutch Renaissance humanist (c. 1466–1536) who made the pilgrimage to Canterbury in 1513 with Dean John Colet and later wrote of an affecting encounter with a beggar outside a Harbledown almshouse.

33. The popular hero Prince Edward (1330–1376) visited St. Thomas's shrine at Canterbury in 1357 and later founded and decorated the chancery in the Cathedral crypt, which is

named after him. As well, a clear spring well behind Lafranc's tower is known as the Black Prince's Well and is supposed by some to have healing powers. Legend has it that on his deathbed, Edward sent for a draught from the well. He is buried in the Chapel of Our Lady in the Undercroft at Canterbury. See Julia Cartwright's "The Pilgrim's Way: VII: Charing to Harbledown," *The Art Journal* (1891): 347–52.

## AN ITALIAN PILGRIMAGE

1.  Charles Godfrey Leland (1824–1903) was Elizabeth's uncle as well as her friend and literary mentor. Leland travelled broadly and made a name for himself as a journalist and folklorist, publishing over twenty books, including the comic *Hans Breitmann about Town: And Other New Ballads* (1869) and several serious works on gypsy culture.

2.  An abbreviated version of the main text appeared in *The Century Magazine* in two parts: "Italy from a Tricycle" 31.5 (Mar. 1886): 643–64, and "Italy, from a Tricycle" 31.6 (Apr. 1886): 839–59. The Pennells mention two additional chapters, not included here. "The Stones of Rome," the title a play off of Ruskin's three-volume *The Stones of Venice* (1851–1853), first appeared in Philip Gilbert Hamerton's *Portfolio* (London: Seeley, 1885): 158–72. The chapter "Vetturino *versus* Tricycle," by Joseph, appeared in *Outing* 6.2 (May 1885): 230–32. See "A Note on the Text," this volume. The "second stage" of their "Pilgrimage to Rome" is recounted in their book *Our Sentimental Journey through France and Italy* (London: Longmans, Green & Co., 1888).

3.  A prefatory "Apology," written with an affected self-deprecating tone, is a literary convention that stretches back to medieval times and was used in John Bunyan's 1678 Christian allegory *The Pilgrim's Progress*. Leland's "Apology" mimics the style and format of Bunyan's, adding some humorous twists.

4.  One of the more popular comic ballads in the *Breitmann* collection was "Schnitzerl's Philosopede," a two-part piece about a buffoonish philosopher's attempt to ride a peculiar velocipede of his own eccentric design. The poem, like all the Breitmann ballads, is written in a kind of caricatured, faux-Germanic dialect. It is, indeed, one of the first known poems about early bicycles.

5.  The American version, *Two Pilgrims' Progress*, includes the following additional lines here:

    > Now, for the Book I something have to say
    > (Pray mark Mee well, good Reader, while you may).
    > They say that in the Publick some there bee
    > Who take it ill 'cause it doth Parody
    > JOHN BUNYAN'S Progress. That can ne'er be said
    > By any who JOHN BUNYAN'S Booke have read,
    > Since he himself protests against the Whim
    > Of those who said the selfsame thing of him,
    > And thought he lightly treated solemn Things.
    > List the Defence which to this Charge he brings:
    > "This Book will make a Traveler of Thee,

"If by its Councill thou will guided be.

"And it is writ in such a Dialect

"As may the Minds of listless Men affect.

"It seems a NOVELTY, and yet contains

"Nothing but sound and honest Gospel Strains."

Now I can make no more Apologie

Than Honest JOHN did make for himself, d'ye see;

6. In John Bunyan's classic Christian allegory *The Pilgrim's Progress from This World to That Which is to Come* (1678), Chapter 14, this is the phrase used by Mr. BY-ENDS to describe the pilgrims Christian and Hopeful, who are on their way to the Celestial City.

7. This thirty-five francs duty is said to have since been abolished through the exertions of the National Cyclists' Union [Pennell's note].

8. A severe cholera epidemic had passed through the area around Naples early in 1884, killing over 14,000 people and causing widespread panic and economic chaos throughout other parts of the country. (So devastating were the spin-off effects of the 1884 cholera epidemic that when another wave hit the country in 1911, government officials attempted to cover it up, so as to not scare off tourists.) The Pennells had postponed their original summer trip because of concerns about cholera. By the fall of the year, it was clear that Tuscany was under no threat, though there were still reports of cholera in some parts of the country. See Frank M. Snowden, *Naples in the Time of Cholera, 1884–1911* (New York: Cambridge UP, 1996).

9. Possibly John Mead Howells (1868–1959), architect son of William Dean Howells, whom Joseph had worked with during his previous trip to Italy.

10. The direct road to Rome starts from the Porta Romana [Pennell's note].

11. Cycling, except under certain restrictions, is now forbidden in Florence. There is a cycling club in the Cascine [Pennell's note]. A ban on cycling within some European cities was common in the 1880s, for reasons related to safety and maintaining traffic flow.

12. Raffaella Sanzio da Urbino (1483–1520) was an Italian painter and architect of the High Renaissance. Pietro Perugino (c. 1450–1523) was an Italian painter of the Umbrian school. Raphael was his most famous pupil.

13. Bell tower, often attached to a church or other public building.

14. Bon voyage.

15. Road from Florence to Empoli, good [Pennell's note].

16. Giovanni Boccaccio (1313–1375), Italian poet, Renaissance humanist, and author of *The Decameron* (1348–1353).

17. Eating house.

18. A ground-level (or occasionally second-level) gallery on the exterior of a building and open to the air on one side.

19. Usually spelled *arrivederla*, a polite form of *arrivederci* or "goodbye" generally used when addressing a single person.

20. Prominent Italian noble families in the Siena area during the Renaissance.

21. Here I am!

22. Publius Vergilius Maro (70 BC–19 BC), ancient Roman poet of the Augustan period, author of *Eclogues*, *Georgics*, and *The Aeneid*.

23. Umberto I (1844–1900), King of Italy from 1878 until his death.

24. Members of Italian military corps that carried out civil police duties.

25. Departing, as in a train leaving the station.

26. Up, up, up.

27. Line 4 (with some minor punctuation changes) of Percy Shelley's poem "Ode to the West Wind" (1820).

28. Loosely translated as "Banditry is forbidden."

29. Pushed down hard on the brake lever.

30. Commonly called skirt guards, these fenders were designed to prevent dresses from getting caught in the chain and thus becoming torn or dirty.

31. Usually spelled "perché," meaning "Why?" in Italian.

32. A line from Ophelia's song in *Hamlet* Act 4, Scene 5. Early editors of Shakespeare, such as William Warburton, pointed out that cockle-shells were an essential badge of pilgrim garb, perhaps representing a distant sea journey. See Warburton's *The Works of Shakespear* [sic] Vol. 8 (Dublin: R. Owen, 1747): 201.

33. A reference to Joseph's earlier visit to Italy with William Dean Howells in 1883.

34. Millard F. Fillmore (1800–1874), thirteenth president of the United States, from 1850 to 1853.

35. Francis M. Crawford (1854–1909), Italian-born American novelist who wrote several novels set in Italy.

36. Samuel Cutler Ward (1814–1884), American poet, author, and gourmet.

37. Bayard Taylor (1825–1878), American poet, critic, and travel writer who travelled extensively in, and wrote about, Europe, Africa, and Asia.

38. Catherine of Siena (1347–1380), philosopher and theologian, one of the two patron saints of Italy (along with St. Francis of Assisi). She claimed to have seen her first vision of Christ when she was five or six years old. Legend has it that one summer or fall day she and her brother Stefano were returning from a visit to her older sister Bonaventura in another part of the city, when she saw a vision in the sky of a smiling Christ and Peter, Paul, and John the Evangelist. See Don Brophy's *Catherine of Siena: A Passionate Life* (New York: Bluebridge, 2010).

39. The Duomo or Cathedral of Siena, completed in the thirteenth century, features an inlaid marble mosaic floor with panels featuring these historical prophet figures. Hermes Trismegistus was an ancient Greek prophet and author of the Hermetic Corpus, sacred texts of Hermeticism.

40. The Black Plague killed about half of the population of 60,000 people in 1348. See Robert Gottfried's *The Black Death: National and Human Disasters in Medieval Europe* (New York: Free Press, 1983).

41. Thirteenth century clubs, *brigate spenderecce*, where "young people purposely wasted their fortunes on the most lavish banquets they could conceive" (The Eminent Martino of Como, *The Art of Cooking: The First Modern Cookery Book*, Ed. Luigi Ballerini, Trans.

Jeremy Parzen (Berkeley: U of California P, 2005): 40. Dante describes one in *The Inferno* 29.125–32.

42. Lano appears in *The Inferno* 13.118–23. See translator Longfellow's note to line 120: "'Lano,' says Boccaccio, *Comento*, 'was a young gentleman of Siena, who had a large patrimony, and associating himself with a club of other young Sienese, called the Spendthrift Club, they also being all rich, together with them, not spending but squandering, in a short time he consumed all that he had and became very poor.' Joining some Florentine troops sent out against the Aretines, he was in a skirmish at the parish of Toppo, which Dante calls a joust; 'and notwithstanding he might have saved himself,' continues Boccaccio, 'remembering his wretched condition, and it seeming to him a grievous thing to bear poverty, as he had been very rich, he rushed into the thick of the enemy and was slain, as perhaps he desired to be.'"

43. Musician/poet of ancient Greek mythology, who was able to charm living things and even stones with his music.

44. The Bridge of Sighs in Venice. Legend has it that lovers who kiss on a gondola at sunset under a bridge will be granted eternal love. It was the source-story of a standard marionette show in Italy in the late nineteenth century. This episode at the marionette show may have been partly inspired by one episode in Robert Louis Stevenson's *Inland Voyage*. In the chapter "Précy and the Marionettes," Stevenson describes a comically bad and chaotic performance.

45. Punch and Judy was a popular traditional English puppet show, performed on the street in a small booth. Its origins are in sixteenth-century Italian *commedia dell'arte*. The name Punch, in fact, derives from the stock Neapolitan puppet character Pulcinella. See George Speaight's *Punch and Judy: A History* (Boston: Plays, Inc., 1955).

46. Street urchin.

47. Little boys.

48. Swiss cigars made by Frossards.

49. Short story "A Tale of Negative Gravity" by American writer and humorist Frank R. Stockton (1834–1902) published in *The Century* (Nov. 1884): 135–43. Stockton later wrote about cycling in *Pomona's Travels* (1894) and *The Bicycle of Cathay* (1900). Joseph had crossed paths with Stockton in Venice in 1883 and later done some illustrating for Stockton's work in *St. Nicholas* magazine (*Life and Letters of Joseph Pennell*, vol. 1: 95, 133).

50. Good night.

51. French song, more commonly "Ah! Que j'aime les militaires," from Jacques Offenbach's opera *La Grande Duchesse de Gerolstein* (1867).

52. Bernardino of Siena (1380–1444), priest, Franciscan missionary, and patron saint of debtors and gambling addicts. According to one story, Bernardino once persuaded a dice carver to switch to carving ivory tablets with the name of Jesus on them. The man then became wealthy.

53. A side-by-side tandem tricycle, as opposed to the front-and-back tricycles favoured by the Pennells. James Starley of Coventry, England, developed the first tandem tricycle in the late 1870s, which he called the Salvo Sociable (Herlihy 210). See introduction.

54. Down, down, down.

55. Thomas the Apostle, also known as Doubting Thomas.

56. Possibly a reference to the Romanian word for tramway, which may have been gypsy slang for a vehicle.

57. Farewell.

58. The wolf, specifically a she-wolf, was an emblem of the confederate cities of Siena. It appears on one of the panels in the mosaic floor of the Duomo.

59. In a later article Elizabeth describes at length the prevalence of Italian "bowls" or *bocce*: "Wherever you go [in Italy], you are sure to see men playing it—in front of all the roadside *osterie*, outside the city walls, in the shady avenues that so often run around them, in whatever green spaces there may be within the city limits" ("Sports at the Home of the Carnival" 583).

60. Flat, level, or gentle.

61. After her mother died, Elizabeth and her sister were placed by their father in the Convent of the Sacred Heart at Torresdale, outside Philadelphia. Elizabeth lived there from age six through sixteen. She writes about this experience in *My Philadelphia* (1914), and her friend Agnes Reppler provides another perspective in her memoir *Our Convent Days* (Boston: Houghton Mifflin, 1905).

62. One of the rest havens for the pilgrims en route to the Celestial City in Bunyan's *Pilgrim's Progress*, Christian sees "a most pleasant mountainous country, beautiful with woods, vineyards, fruits of all sorts; flowers also, with springs and fountains, very delectable to behold" (37).

63. White garb was one of the habits of Benedictine monks.

64. This chapter may have been at least partly inspired by an episode in Robert Louis Stevenson's *Travels with a Donkey in the Cévennes*. In a section titled "Our Lady of the Snows," Stevenson recounts his brief stay at a Trappist monastery, describing the various monks and boarders he encounters there.

65. Renaissance painter (c. 1445–1523) born in Cortona.

66. Painter Giovanni Antonio Bazzi (1477–1549), also known as Il Sodoma.

67. A type of earthenware with coloured decoration and a white glaze.

68. Theocritus was a Greek poet from the third century BC, credited with inventing bucolic poetry. Percy Shelley (1792–1822), Romantic poet, spent time in Italy and wrote several pastoral poems, including the elegy "Adonais" (1821) in honour of poet John Keats.

69. Lewis Carroll's *Alice in Wonderland* (1865).

70. The trans-alpine railway, through parts of Switzerland and Italy, was constructed in the 1870s, and was notorious for its twists, turns, and tunnels.

71. Canto 1. lines 28–30 of Henry Wadsworth Longfellow's 1867 translation of *The Inferno* (Champaign, IL: Project Gutenberg, 1999):

> After my weary body I had rested,
> The way resumed I on the desert slope,
> So that the firm foot ever was the lower.

72. See *Georgics*, Book 2, where Virgil discusses techniques of arboculture and viniculture.

> Olive trees fare best when grown on the trunk, vines by that practice
> we've named layering, Paphian myrtles best from solid stems;
> from slips, the healthy hazel, the mighty ash,
> and the poplar out of which Hercules once made himself a garland,
> just like the sacred oaks, the sky-high palm,
> and the fir ahead of which lie disasters of the deep. (lines 63–68).

73. Public stagecoach, especially as used in France in the eighteenth century.
74. In *New Italian Sketches* by John Addington Symonds (1840–1893), British writer and scholar, published in 1884.
75. In 1869, Thomas Humber, of Nottingham, founded the Humber Bicycle Company, one of the earliest English manufacturers of bicycles and tricycles. The Humber tandem tricycle, like the one the Pennells rode in Italy, was a popular model in the mid-1880s. In her *Life and Letters of Joseph Pennell*, Elizabeth explains that "before leaving London we had exchanged the Coventry Rotary [which they had used on the Canterbury trip] for a Humber tandem, a better designed, better looking machine, and it did not fail us from beginning to end" (vol. 1: 129).
76. Speedwell Club, one of the oldest cycling clubs in England, founded in 1876.
77. Waiter.
78. See *Inferno* translator Longfellow's note at 29.046: "The Val di Chiana, near Arezzo, was in Dante's time marshy and pestilential. Now, by the effect of drainage, it is one of the most beautiful and fruitful of the Tuscan valleys."
79. Foreigners.
80. That's very kind of you!
81. Road from Montepulciano to Cortona good and generally level—long coast out of the former, three miles' climb into the latter [Pennell's note].
82. Probably Robert Vischer's *Luca Signorelli und die italienische Renaissance: eine kunsthistorische Monographie* (Leipzig: Veit, 1879).
83. See *Georgics*, Book 1:

> What can I tell about the storms of autumn and its signs,
> or, even, when the days are closing down and summer sun's abating,
> what then must men beware of? Or, say, when spring comes tumbling
> down in showers and crops of corn are tall already,
> their green stalks standing proud with sap?
> How often I have seen, just as the farmer's driven in to reap
> the flaxen field and top the fragile barley crop,
> the clash of squalls and gales in battle mode
> as they ripped up from roots the swathes of ripe and ready corn
> and held them up, the way malefic whirlwinds
> toss beardless stalks around the place, hither and yon.

At other times a rush of water cascades from the sky,
   clouds spill their mass into the foul darkness of a deluge,
   as the heavens open and the rainfall wipes the smiles
   off the faces of the crop the oxen worked so hard to make.
   Ditches to the brim, rampant channels overflow,
   the sea rampaging up each boiling inlet.
         Then Jupiter, squire of the sky, straddling the night clouds, dispatches
   from his gleaming hand a thunderbolt and makes the whole world quake.
   Wild beasts take off, and everywhere human hearts
   are laid low in a panic. He hurls that blazing dart
   onto Athos, Rhodope, and the peaks of Ceraunia;
   south winds redouble and rains intensify;
   now the great groves in the gale, and now the shores, burst into tears. (lines 311–34)

84. Poor little thing.

85. Picaresque novel (published 1715–1735) by French writer Alain-René Lesage (1668–1747).

86. Descendant of the once powerful Florentine family, rival of the Medicis.

87. Very fair road from Cortona to Perugia; but the new one, Cortona—Castiglione del Lago Perugia—though longer, is more level and easier going [Pennell's note].

88. Raphael's painting "The Deposition" (1507) also known as "Pala Baglione, Borghese Deposition" or "The *Entombment*," was commissioned by Atalanta Baglioni, matriarch of the powerful Baglioni family that controlled Perugia. The painting commemorates the death of her son Grifonetto, who in 1500 was killed while trying to assassinate several members of the Baglioni family. Raphael was twelve years old, a student of Pietro Perugino, at the time of this incident.

89. Also members of the Baglioni family, heroes of a 1495 battle, murdered in 1500.

90. Sister towns of Chatham and Rochester were where Dickens spent some of the happiest years of his childhood between 1817 and 1823. These places form part of the setting for some of Dickens's best-known novels (*Pickwick Papers, Great Expectations, The Mystery of Edwin Drood*).

91. In Nathaniel Hawthorne's *The Marble Faun, Or the Romance of Monte Beni* (1860), Miriam and Donatello (and their American friend Kenyon) meet under this statue of Julius in Perugia following Donatello's murder of a mysterious man who had threatened Miriam. At the end of Chapter 35: The Bronze Pontiff's Benediction, the narrator says, "At this moment it so chanced that all the three friends by one impulse glanced upward at the statue of Pope Julius; and there was the majestic figure stretching out the hand of benediction over them, and bending down upon this guilty and repentant pair its visage of grand benignity" (Hawthorne, vol. 6: 371). Elizabeth says this is Pope Julius II but it is, in fact, Pope Julius III. Thanks to Paola Malpezzi Price for this correction.

92. Fra Egidio (Brother Giles of Asissi) (1190–1262) was one of the original companions of St. Francis of Assisi.

93. The frescoes cycle on the upper church at Assisi, depicting scenes from the life of St. Francis, have traditionally been attributed to Florentine painter Giotto di Bondone (1266/67–1337), though art historians now doubt the attribution.

94. American feminist and medical doctor (1832–1919) who volunteered during the American Civil War.

95. Clitumnus is one of the possible birthplaces of Virgil and it is described fondly in his *Georgics* 2: 146–48.

> From here, Clitumnus, came the washed-white and the bull that was
> primed for the sacrifice, those animals that often bathed in your holy waters
> and drew to the temples of the gods throngs who celebrated Roman triumphs.

96. See Pliny's *Epistulae* VII: 8.

97. In Canto 3 of *The Inferno*, Virgil and Dante, at the Gates of Hell, hear innumerable voices of torment and suffering, in strange and foreign dialects, from the souls of those who didn't commit to good or evil but rather avoided making a clear moral choice.

> There sighs, complaints, and ululations loud
> Resounded through the air without a star,
> Whence I, at the beginning, wept thereat.
> Languages diverse, horrible dialects,
> Accents of anger, words of agony,
> And voices high and hoarse, with sound of hands,
> Made up a tumult that goes whirling on
> For ever in that air for ever black,
> Even as the sand doth, when the whirlwind breathes. (lines 22–30)

98. Italian infantry soldiers recognizable by plumed hats.

99. Commonly used term for the first-generation of velocipedes manufactured in the 1860s, featuring wooden wheels of roughly equal size, with pedals attached to the front wheel. The notoriously rough ride gave rise to the "boneshaker" nickname.

100. The Pennells and some of their contemporaries enjoyed mocking the large contingent of cycle-racers or "Scorchers" who, from the earliest days of the velocipede, used the machines for racing and various attempts at setting speed and distance records.

101. A type of porous rock.

102. See Book 7: Epigram 93 of *The Epigrams of Martial* (Marcus Valerius Martialis). The Latin poet (40–c. 102) begs the town of Narnia to send back his friend Quintus Ovidius, and not detain him any longer from his Nomentum farm, near Martial's own:

> Narnia, circled by your river white with sulphurous flood, hard of access on your double ridge, why do you like to take my Quintus away from me so often and keep him so lengthily detained? Why do you destroy for me the reason for my little place at Nomentum, which was valuable because of my neighbour? Come now, spare me, Narnia, and don't overdo it with Quintus; so may it be yours to enjoy your bridge for ever.

103. Gothic German painter, engraver, and wood-cut artist, one of the earliest European landscape artists.

104. This mountain peak, about twenty miles north of Rome, is mentioned in *Odes of Horace* 1.9.

> Do you see how Sorácte stands clothed white
> in layers of snow and struggling boughs sustain
> their load no longer, while from piercing
> cold the rivers have stopped flowing? (lines 1–4)

105. Literally "Brother Devil," the popular name given to Michele Pezza (1771–1806), a Neapolitan bandit leader fought the French occupation of Naples.
106. Angelo Ambrogini (1454–1494), Italian Renaissance scholar and poet, composer of lyric poetry.
107. Pastoral figures in Virgil's "Eclogue 7."
108. In Christ!
109. On arriving in Rome in October 1884, the Pennells decided to stay the winter, despite worries about the health of Joseph's father back in Philadelphia (*LL1*: 130). Joseph continued sketching cathedrals and Elizabeth wrote a variety of magazine articles on Italian art and culture, all while they socialized with ex-pat American and British writers and artists. In the early spring they travelled to Venice, where they stayed until May, before returning to London.

# Works Cited

Arnold, Matthew. *Culture and Anarchy: An Essay in Political and Social Criticism*. 1869.
Ed. and with introduction by Jane Garnett. Oxford: Oxford UP, 2006.

Booth, Bradford A., and Ernest Mehew, eds. *The Letters of Robert Louis Stevenson*. Vol. 5.
New Haven, CT: Yale UP, 1995.

Bunyan, John. *The Pilgrim's Progress in the Similitude of a Dream*. Cardinalis Etext Press.
1993. Web.

"A Canterbury Pilgrimage." *Outing* 6.3. (Sep. 1885): 321–28.

Clarke, Meaghan. *Critical Voices: Women and Art Criticism in Britain 1880–1905*. Burlington, VT:
Ashgate, 2005.

"Current Literature." [Rev. of *A Canterbury Pilgrimage*.] *Daily Evening Bulletin* (3 Oct. 1885).
Column E.

"Cycle and Camera." *The Penny Illustrated Paper* (8 Mar. 1890), 154.

Dickens, Charles, Jr. *Dictionary of the Thames*. London: Macmillan & Co., 1879, 1886.

"From Coventry to Chester on Wheels." *The Century Magazine* 28.5 (Sep. 1884): 643–55.

Dante. *The Inferno*. Trans. Henry Wadsworth Longfellow. 1867. Champaign, IL:
Project Gutenberg, 1999. Web.

Dodge, Pryor. *The Bicycle*. Paris: Flammarion, 1996.

Egbert, Victor. *Checklist of Books and Contributions to Books by Joseph and Elizabeth Robins Pennell*.
Philadelphia: Free Library of Philadelphia, 1945.

Keppel, Frederick. *Joseph Pennell: Etcher, Illustrator, Author*. New York: Keppel, 1907.

Kron, Karl. [Lyman Hotchkiss Bagg] *Ten Thousand Miles on a Bicycle*. New York: Karl Kron, 1887.
Reprint. New York: Emil Rosenblatt, 1982.

Hawes, Louis. *Presences of Nature: British Landscape, 1780–1830*. New Haven, CT: Yale Center
for British Art, 1982.

Hawthorne, Nathaniel. *Complete Works of Nathaniel Hawthorne*. Ed. Boston: Houghton Mifflin,
1883.

Herlihy, David V. *Bicycle: The History*. New Haven, CT: Yale UP, 2004.

Horace. *Odes of Horace*. Trans. Jeffrey H. Kaimowitz and Ronnie Ancona. Baltimore, MD:
Johns Hopkins UP, 2008.

"Light Travel." *The Atlantic,* 59 (1887): 700–01.

"Literary Review [of *A Canterbury Pilgrimage*]." *The Congregationalist* (13 Aug. 1885): 6.

Martial. *The Epigrams of Martial.* Vol. 2. Trans. D.R. Shackleton Bailey. Loeb Classical Library. London: Harvard UP, 1993.

Norcliffe, Glen. "On the Technical and Social Significance of the Tricycle." *Cycle History 17: Proceedings of the Seventeenth International Cycle History Conference,* Ed. Glen Norcliffe (San Francisco: Van der Plas, 2007) 59–68.

"One Hundred Books of Sport." *Outing* 9.5 (Feb. 1887): 478–80.

Pennell, Elizabeth Robins. *Charles Godfrey Leland.* 2 Volumes. Boston: Houghton Mifflin, 1906.

———. *The Life and Letters of Joseph Pennell.* 2 Volumes. Boston: Little, Brown, 1929.

_____. *London Diaries, 1884–1892.* Unpublished. Harry Ransom Center. University of Texas at Austin. Austin, TX.

———. *Our House and London Out Our Windows.* Boston: Houghton Mifflin, 1912.

———. *Our Philadelphia.* Philadelphia: J.B. Lippincott, 1914.

———. *Our Sentimental Journey through France and Italy.* New edition with appendix. London: T. Fisher Unwin, 1893.

_____. "Sports at the Home of the Carnival" *Outing* 9.6 (Mar. 1887): 580–87.

———. "Twenty Years of Cycling." *Fortnightly Review* 68 (62 (n.s.)): (Aug. 1897): 188–97.

Pennell, Joseph, and Elizabeth Robins Pennell. *A Canterbury Pilgrimage.* London: Seeley, 1885.

———. *An Italian Pilgrimage.* London: Seeley, 1887.

_____. *Pennell-Whistler Collection,* Special Collections, Library of Congress, Washington, DC, boxes 305, 307.

Pennell, Joseph, and Elizabeth Robins. *Two Pilgrims' Progress: From Fair Florence to the Eternal City of Rome.* Boston: Roberts Brothers, 1886/87.

Pennell, Joseph. *Adventures of an Illustrator.* Boston: Little, Brown, 1925.

Rev. of Lord Bury's *Cycling Handbook. The Pall Mall Gazette* (20 May 1887): 5.

Rev. of *A Canterbury Pilgrimage. The Graphic* (29 Aug. 1885): 247.

Rev. of *An Italian Pilgrimage. Daily News* (16 Dec. 1886): 3.

Rev. of *An Italian Pilgrimage. The York Herald* (22 Jan. 1887): 5.

Robins, Edward. "Philadelphiana." *Colophon. New Graphic Series* 2 (June 1939): 17–22.

Slater, Michael. *Charles Dickens.* New Haven, CT: Yale UP, 2009.

Tebbel, John, and Mary Ellen Zuckerman. *The Magazine in America, 1741–1990.* Oxford: Oxford UP, 1991.

Tinker, Edward Larocque. *The Pennells.* New York: New York Public Library, 1951.

Tucker, Amy. *Illustration and the Master: Henry James and the Magazine Revolution.* Palo Alto, CA: Stanford UP, 2010.

Virgil. *Georgics.* Trans. Peter Fallon. Oxford: Oxford UP, 2006. Web.

Watson, Nicola J. *The Literary Tourist: Readers and Places in Romantic and Victorian Britain.* London: Palgrave Macmillan, 2006.

Williams, Jacqueline Block. Introduction. *The Delights of Delicate Eating.* By Elizabeth Robins Pennell. U of Illinois P, 2000. vii–xxv.

# Bibiography

## SELECTED EARLY CYCLE-TRAVEL LITERATURE TO 1900

This bibliography includes only book-length volumes. Thanks to Duncan R. Jamieson (Ph.D., Professor of History, Ashland University, Ashland, Ohio) for granting permission to adapt this bibliography from his Bicycle Travel and Touring Resources, Chronological Bibliography.

Allen, Thomas Gaskell, Jr., and William Lewis Sachtleben. *Across Asia on a Bicycle: The Journey of Two American Students from Constantinople to Peking.* New York: The Century Co., 1894.

Boddy, the Rev. Alexander A. *Days in Galilee and Scenes in Judea.* London: Gay & Bird, 1900.

Callan, Hugh. *From the Clyde to the Jordan.* New York: Charles Scribner's Sons, 1895.

———. *Wanderings on Wheel and on Foot through Europe.* London: Sampson Low, Marston, Searle & Rivington, 1887.

Cavan, Frederick Edward Gould Lambart (9th Earl of Cavan). *With the Yacht, Camera and Cycle in the Mediterranean.* London: Sampson Low, Marston & Co., 1895.

Chandler, Alfred D., and John C. Sharp. *A Bicycle Tour in England and Wales.* Boston: A. Williams & Co., 1881.

Chilosa (pseudonym). *Waif and Stray: The Adventures of Two Tricycles.* Westminster: The Roxburghe Press, 1895.

Cole, Grenville A.J. *The Gypsy Road: A Journey from Krakow to Coblentz.* London: Macmillan, 1894.

Edwardes, Charles. *In Jutland with a Cycle.* London: Chapman and Hall, Ltd., 1897.

Elwell, F.A. *The Elwell European Bicycle Tours.* Portland, ME: F.A. Elwell, 1895.

Eric, Allan (pseudonym for C.W. Willis), and The "Junior Partner." *Following the Tow-path and through the Adirondacks Awheel.* Boston: N.E.R.G. Publishing Co., 1898.

———. *Montreal by Way of Chazy and Down the St. Lawrence River to Quebec.* Boston: Geo. R. Willis & Co., 1899.

Fraser, John Foster. *Round the World on a Wheel: Being the Narrative of a Bicycle Ride of Nineteen Thousand Two Hundred and Thirty-Seven Miles through Seventeen Countries and across Three Continents by John Foster Fraser, S. Edward Lunn and F.H. Lowe.* London: Methuen & Co., 1899.

Freeston, Charles L. *Cycling in the Alps, with Some Notes on the Chief Passes.* Drawings by A.R. Quinton. London: Grant Richards, 1900.

Garrison, Winfred Ernest. *Wheeling through Europe*. St. Louis: Christian Publishing Co., 1900.

Golder, S. *A Tandem Tour in Norway*. London: Iliffe, 1888.

Joyce, Weston St. John. *Rambles around Dublin*. Dublin: Printed at the Office of the Evening Telegraph, 1887.

Jefferson, Robert Louis. *Across Siberia on a Bicycle*. London: The Cycle Press, 1896.

———. *Awheel to Moscow and Back: The Record of a Record Cycle Ride*. Preface by Lt. Col. A.R. Saville. London: Sampson Low, Marston & Co., 1895.

———. *A New Ride to Khiva*. London: Methuen and Co., 1899.

———. *Through a Continent on Wheels*. London: Simpkin, Marshall, Hamilton, Kent & Co., Ltd., 1899.

———. *To Constantinople on a Bicycle: The Story of My Ride*. London: The Cycle Press, 1894.

Jerome, Jerome K. *Three Men on the Bummel*. Oxford: Oxford UP, 1998 (1900).

Kron, Karl [Lyman Hotchkiss Bagg]. *Ten Thousand Miles on a Bicycle*. New York: University Building, 1887.

McCray, Florine Thayer, and Esther Louise Smith. *Wheels and Whims: An Etching*. Boston: Cupples, Upham, 1884.

McIlrath, H. Darwin. *Around the World on Wheels for the Inter Ocean: The Travels and Adventures in Foreign Lands of Mr. and Mrs. H. Darwin McIlrath*. Chicago: Inter Ocean Publishing Co., 1898.

Nauticus [Reade, Charles Edward]. *Nauticus in Scotland: A Tricycle Tour of 2462 miles including Skye and the West Coast*. London: Simkin, Marshall & Co., 1883.

———. *Nauticus on his Hobby Horse: Or the Adventures of a Sailor during a Tricycle Cruise of 1427 Miles*. London: William Ridgeway, 1880.

Peard, F.F. *A Summer's Cycling Reminiscence: The Story of a Three Months Bicycling Tour through Europe and an Account of Some of the Impressions Received*. By one of the party. Toronto: Press of "Cycling," 1891.

Pennell, Elizabeth Robins. Illustrated by Joseph Pennell. *To Gipsyland*. London: T. Fisher Irwin, 1893.

Pennell, Joseph, and Elizabeth Robins. *A Canterbury Pilgrimage*. New York: Charles Scribner's Sons, 1885.

———. *An Italian Pilgrimage*. London: Seeley & Co., 1887. Published in the United States as *Two Pilgrims' Progress: From Fair Florence to the Eternal City of Rome*. Boston: Roberts Brothers, 1886.

———. *Our Sentimental Journey through France and Italy*. London: Longmans, Green & Co., 1888.

———. *Over the Alps on a Bicycle*. London: T. Fisher Unwin, 1898.

Simonin, C.F.A. *A Pedaller Abroad: Being an Illustrated Narrative of the Adventures and Experiences of a Cycling Twain during a 1,000 Kilometre Ride in and around Switzerland*. London: J. Caustin, 1897.

Stevens, Thomas. *Around the World on a Bicycle. Volume I. From San Francisco to Teheran*. London: Century, 1888.

———. *Around the World on a Bicycle. Volume II. From Teheran to Yokohama*. New York: Charles Scribner's Sons, 1888.

Thayer, George B. *Pedal and Path: Across the Continent Awheel and Afoot.* Hartford, CT: Evening Post Association, 1887.

Thwaites, Rueben Gold. *Our Cycling Tour in England, from Canterbury to Dartmoor Forest, and Back by Way of Bath, Oxford and the Thames Valley.* Chicago: A.C. McClurg, 1892.

Winder, Tom W. *Around the United States by Bicycle.* Elmira, NY: Tom Winder, Publisher, 1895.

Workman, Fanny B., and William Hunter. *Algerian Memories: A Bicycle Tour over the Atlas to the Sahara.* New York: Anson D.F. Randolph & Co., 1895.

———. *Sketches Awheel in Modern Iberia.* New York: G.P. Putnam's Sons, 1897.

*Yankee Schoolboys Abroad; Or, the New England Bicycle Club in Scotland, England, and Paris. July–September, 1892.* Brookline, MA: C.A.W. Spencer, 1893.

## THE PENNELLS' CYCLING PUBLICATIONS

This chronological bibliography includes cycling-related works published by one or both of the Pennells. The original byline is provided for each piece, though attributing true authorship is tricky with the Pennells since they often wrote collaboratively. This list does not include the Pennells' considerable anonymously or pseudonymously published cycling journalism, such as the weekly anonymous contributions to *The Pall Mall Gazette*'s "Cycling Notes" between January 1894 and December 1895, that were almost certainly written by them. The list does, however, include two items (indicated by *) published without their names for which we have proof of authorship.

"From Coventry to Chester on Wheels." *The Century Magazine* 28.5 (Sep. 1884): 643–55. [In The Life and Letters of Joseph Pennell, Elizabeth claims authorship of this unsigned piece (1: 106).]*

Joseph Pennell. "In Italy. Vetturino *versus* Tricycle." *Outing* 6.2 (May 1885): 230–32.

Joseph Pennell. "With the Veloce Club to Ostia." *Outing* 6.3 (June 1885): 259–64.

Joseph and Elizabeth Robins Pennell. *A Canterbury Pilgrimage.* London: Seeley, 1885. Published in the United States in New York: Charles Scribner's Sons, 1885.

"A Canterbury Pilgrimage." *Outing* 6.6 (Sep. 1885): 725–30. [This unsigned piece is a short review that includes a lengthy excerpt from the Pennells' book of the same name.]

Joseph Pennell. "My Scorch to Ripley." *Outing* 7.3 (Dec. 1885): 315–18.

Elizabeth Robins Pennell. "Italy from a Tricycle, Part 1." *The Century Magazine* 31.5 (Mar. 1886): 644–64.

Joseph Pennell. "Italian Notes." *Outing* 7.6 (Mar. 1886): 677–81.

Elizabeth Robins Pennell. "Italy, from a Tricycle, Part 2." *The Century Magazine* 31.6 (Apr. 1886): 839–59.

Joseph and Elizabeth Robins Pennell. *An Italian Pilgrimage.* London: Seeley, 1887. Published in the United States as *Two Pilgrims' Progress: From Fair Florence, to the Eternal City of Rome.* Boston: Roberts Bros., 1886/87.

Joseph Pennell. "The Stanley Show." *Outing* 9 (May 1886): 137–46.

Joseph Pennell. "After Dick Turpin on a Tricycle.—I." *The Pall Mall Gazette* 6729 (9 Oct. 1886): 5.

Joseph Pennell. "After Dick Turpin on a Tricycle.—II." *The Pall Mall Gazette* 6740 (22 Oct. 1886): 5.

Joseph Pennell. "Dick Turpin's Visit to the Gypsies." *The Pall Mall Gazette* 6744 (27 Oct. 1886): 5.

Joseph Pennell. "Coming Cycles at the Stanley Show." *The Pall Mall Gazette* 6822 (27 Jan. 1887): 5.

Joseph Pennell. "Cycles at the Stanley Show." *The Pall Mall Gazette* 7139 (2 Feb. 1888): 5.

Joseph Pennell. "How to Cycle in France on Seven Francs a Day." *The Pall Mall Gazette* 7384
     (15 Nov. 1888): 3.

Joseph and Elizabeth Robins Pennell. *Our Sentimental Journey through France and Italy.*
     London: Longmans, Green & Co., 1888.

Joseph Pennell. "How to Cycle in Europe." *Outing* 13 (Mar. 1889): 511–14.

Elizabeth Robins Pennell. Sketches by Joseph Pennell. "To the Paris Exhibition on a Tandem
     Bicycle." *The Graphic* (22 June 1889): n.p.

Elizabeth Robins Pennell. "Outings for Thin Pocket-Books." *The Chautauquan* 9 (July 1889):
     571–74.

N.C.U. "Cycle & Camera." *The Penny Illustrated Paper and Illustrated Times* (1 June 1889–25
     Nov. 1893). [The Pennells wrote some, if not all, of these weekly cycling columns, which
     appeared almost every Saturday in *The Penny Illustrated Paper*. The pieces were unsigned
     or signed only with the initials N.C.U., probably for National Cyclists' Union, but
     Elizabeth and Joseph refer to themselves by name in some of the columns.]*

Elizabeth Robins Pennell. "From Cathedral to Cathedral. First Paper." *The Chautauquan* 9
     (n.s. 2) (1890): 76–80.

Elizabeth Robins Pennell. "From Cathedral to Cathedral. Second Paper." *The Chautauquan* 9
     (n.s. 2) (1890): 186–90.

Elizabeth Robins Pennell. "From Cathedral to Cathedral. Third Paper." *The Chautauquan* 9
     (n.s. 2) (1890): 321–25.

Elizabeth Robins Pennell. "Cycling." *St. Nicholas: An Illustrated Magazine for Young Folks.*
     17 (July 1890): 732–40.

Joseph Pennell. "Cycling: Past, Present, and Future." *New Review* 4 (Feb. 1891): 171–80.

Elizabeth Robins Pennell. "From Berlin to Buda Pest on a Bicycle." *The London Illustrated News*
     (Published in twelve parts between Apr. 23 and Aug. 27, 1892).

Elizabeth Robins Pennell. Pictures by Joseph Pennell. "To Gipsyland." *The Century Magazine*
     45.1 (Nov. 1892): 109–21.

Elizabeth Robins Pennell. Pictures by Joseph Pennell. "To Gipsyland." *The Century Magazine*
     45.2 (Dec. 1892): 258–71.

J. and E.R. Pennell. "The Most Picturesque Place in the World." *The Century Magazine* 46.45
     (July 1893): 345–51.

Elizabeth Robins Pennell. Pictures by Joseph Pennell. "To Gipsyland." *The Century Magazine*
     45.3 (Jan. 1893): 414–25.

Elizabeth Robins Pennell. Illustrated by Joseph Pennell. *To Gipsyland.* London: T. Fisher Irwin,
     1893.

Mrs. E. Robins Pennell. "Cycling." *In Ladies in the Field: Sketches of Sport.* Ed. The Lady Greville.
     New York: D. Appleton & Co., 1894. 247–65.

Joseph Pennell and Elizabeth Robins Pennell. "Twenty Years of Cycling." *Fortnightly Review*
     68 (62 n.s.) (Aug. 1897): 191.

Elizabeth Robins Pennell. "Around London by Bicycle." *Harper's New Monthly Magazine*
     95 (Sep. 1897): 489–510.

Elizabeth Robins Pennell. Pictures by Joseph Pennell. "Over the Alps on a Bicycle."
*The Century Magazine* 55.6 (Apr. 1898): 837–52.

Elizabeth Robins Pennell. Illustrated by Joseph Pennell. *Over the Alps on a Bicycle*. London:
T. Fisher Unwin, 1898.

Joseph Pennell. "Cycles and Cycling: Some Notes on the Shows." *Fortnightly Review* 69 (n.s. 63)
(Jan. 1898): 57–67.

Joseph Pennell. "How to Cycle in Europe." *Harper's Monthly Magazine* 96 (Apr. 1898): 880–92.

Joseph Pennell. "In Andalusia with a Bicycle." *The Contemporary Review* 123 (May 1898): 714–26.

Joseph Pennell. "Cycles and Cycling." *Fortnightly Review* 71 (n.s. 65) (Jan. 1899): 110–23.

Joseph Pennell. "The Welsh Cornice." *The Contemporary Review* 75 (Apr. 1899): 522–30.

Elizabeth Robins Pennell. "One Way to See the Paris Exposition." *Lippincott's Monthly Magazine*
65 (May 1900): 777–83.

Joseph Pennell. "Other Things and Improvements in Cycles." *The Contemporary Review* 77
(Jan. 1900): 61–73.

Joseph Pennell. "Cycles and Motors in 1900." *The Contemporary Review* 68 (Jan. 1901): 98–108.

Elizabeth Robins Pennell. Sketches by Joseph Pennell. "Italy's Garden of Eden." *The Century
Magazine* (Oct. 1901): 836–50.

Elizabeth Robins Pennell. "The Italy of Virgil and Horace." *Harper's Monthly Magazine* 104.624
(May 1902): 867–74.

Joseph Pennell. *The Adventures of an Illustrator*. Boston: Little, Brown & Company, 1925.

## NON-CYCLING BOOKS BY THE PENNELLS

This chronological bibliography includes non-cycling books written by one or both of the
Pennells. It does not include books only illustrated by Joseph Pennell but written by someone
other than Elizabeth, nor does it include books that consist solely of illustrations by Joseph
(unless there is an accompanying introduction by Elizabeth). For a more comprehensive list
of all books featuring contributions of any kind (writing and/or illustration) by the Pennells,
see Victor Egbert's *Checklist of Books and Contributions to Books by Joseph and Elizabeth Robins
Pennell*. Philadelphia: Free Library of Philadelphia, 1945.

Elizabeth Robins Pennell. *Life of Mary Wollstonecraft*. Boston: Roberts Brothers, 1884.
Re-issued as *Mary Wollstonecraft*. 1890. Published in England as *Mary Wollstonecraft
Godwin*. London: W.H. Allen & Co., 1885.

Joseph and Elizabeth Robins Pennell. *Our Journey to the Hebrides*. New York: Harper & Bros.,
1889.

Joseph Pennell. *Pen Drawing and Pen Draughtsmen*. London: T.F. Unwin; New York: Macmillan,
1889.

Joseph and Elizabeth Robins Pennell. *Stream of Pleasure: A Narrative of a Journey on the Thames
from Oxford to London. Together with a Practical Chapter by J.G. Legge*. London: T. Fisher
Unwin, 1891.

Joseph and Elizabeth Robins Pennell. *Play in Provence. Being a Series of Sketches Written and
Drawn by Joseph and Elizabeth Robins Pennell*. New York: The Century, 1892.

Joseph Pennell. *Modern Illustration*. London/New York: G. Bell, 1895.

Elizabeth Robins Pennell. *Tantallon Castle*. Edinburgh: T. & A. Constable, 1895.

Elizabeth Robins Pennell. *The Feasts of Autolycus: The Diary of a Greedy Woman*. London: J. Lane,
   1896; New York: Merriam, 1896. Re-issued as *The Delights of Delicate Eating*. Chicago:
   Saalfield, 1900. Re-issued as *A Guide for the Greedy*. Philadelphia: Lippincott, 1923.
   Re-issued as *The Delights of Delicate Eating*. Ed. and Introduction by Jacqueline Block
   Williams. Champaign, IL: U of Illinois P, 2000.

Joseph Pennell. *The Work of Charles Keene*. New York: R.H. Russell, 1897.

Joseph Pennell and Elizabeth Robins Pennell. *Lithography and Lithographers; Some Chapters in
   the History of the Art, together with Descriptions and Technical Explanations of Modern Artistic
   Methods by Joseph Pennell*. New York: Macmillan, 1898. [Revised edition issued in 1915
   with historical parts re-written, a technical section added, and the order of authors'
   names reversed.]

Joseph Pennell. *Concerning the Etchings of Mr. Whistler*. New York: Frederick Keppel, 1899.

Elizabeth Robins Pennell. *Some Interesting Things about Art at the Paris Exposition*. Boston:
   Noyes & Platt, 1900.

Elizabeth Robins Pennell. *My Cookery Books*. Boston, New York: Houghton Mifflin, 1903.

Elizabeth Robins Pennell. *Charles Godfrey Leland: A Biography*. 2 vols. Boston: Houghton
   Mifflin, 1906.

E.R. and J. Pennell. *The Life of James McNeill Whistler*. Philadelphia: Lippincott; London:
   Heinemann, 1908.

Elizabeth Robins Pennell. *Our House and the People in It*. Boston: Houghton Mifflin, 1910.
   [Also published as *Our Home and London out our Windows*, with illustrations by Joseph
   Pennell. Boston: Houghton Mifflin, 1912.]

Elizabeth Robins Pennell. Illustrated by Joseph Pennell. *French Cathedrals, Monasteries, and
   Abbeys, and Sacred Sites of France. Illustrated with 183 pictures by Joseph Pennell, also with
   Plans and Diagrams*. New York: Century, 1910.

Elizabeth Robins Pennell. *Our Philadelphia, described by Elizabeth Robins Pennell, illustrated
   with one-hundred-and five lithographs by Joseph Pennell*. Philadelphia, London:
   J.B. Lippincott, 1914.

Elizabeth Robins Pennell. *Nights: Rome, Venice, in the Aesthetic Eighties; London, Paris, in the
   Fighting Nineties; with Sixteen Illustrations*. Philadelphia, London: J.B. Lippincott, 1916.

Elizabeth Robins Pennell. *The Lovers*. London: W. Heinemann, 1917.

Joseph Pennell. *Etchers and Etching*. New York: Macmillan, 1919. London: T.F. Unwin, 1920.

*The Joseph and Elizabeth Robins Pennell Collection of Whistleriana*. Catalogue Compiled by Joseph
   and Elizabeth Robins Pennell. Washington, DC: Govt. Print Off., 1921.

Pennell, E.R. & J. *The Whistler Journal*. Philadelphia: J.B. Lippincott, 1921.

Elizabeth Robins Pennell. *A Guide for the Greedy, by a Greedy Woman: Being a New and Revised
   Edition of The Feasts of Autolycus*. Philadelphia: J.B. Lippincott, 1923.

Joseph Pennell. *The Adventures of an Illustrator*. Boston: Little, Brown; London: T.F. Unwin, 1925.

Joseph Pennell. Introduction by Elizabeth Robins Pennell. *Joseph Pennell's Pictures of
   Philadelphia: Reproductions of Sixty-four Lithographs Made by Him*. Philadelphia: J.B.
   Lippincott, 1926.

Elizabeth Robins Pennell. *Joseph Pennell: An Account by His Wife, Issued on the Occasion of a Memorial Exhibition of His Works*. New York: Metropolitan Museum of Art, 1926.

Elizabeth Robins Pennell, *Italy's Garden of Eden, with Illustrations by Joseph Pennell*. Philadelphia: Pennell Club, 1927.

Elizabeth Robins Pennell with Joseph Pennell. *The Art of Whistler, with 32 Reproductions in Aquatone Process*. New York: The Modern Library, 1928.

Elizabeth Robins Pennell. *The Life and Letters of Joseph Pennell*. 2 vols. Boston: Little, Brown, 1929.

Elizabeth Robins Pennell. *Whistler the Friend, with Twenty Illustrations*. Philadelphia, London: J.B. Lippincott, 1930.

Pennell, Joseph. *Etchings*. With an introduction by Elizabeth Robins Pennell. New York: Keppel, 1931.

# Index

## Other Titles from The University of Alberta Press

### Conrad Kain

*Letters from a Wandering Mountain Guide, 1906–1933*
CONRAD KAIN
*Edited and with an Introduction by* ZAC ROBINSON
MARIA KOCH & JOHN KOCH, *Translators*
CHIC SCOTT, *Foreword*

Mountain Cairns: A series on the history and culture of the
    Canadian Rockies
512 pages | 30 B&W photographs, 3 maps, notes, bibliography, index
978-1-77212-004-2 | $34.95 paper
978-1-77212-016-5 | $27.99 EPUB
978-1-77212-017-2 | $27.99 Kindle
978-1-77212-018-9 | $27.99 PDF
Mountain Studies | Canadian History | Biography

### Woman Behind the Painter

*The Diaries of Rosalie, Mrs. James Clarke Hook*
ROSALIE HOOK
*Edited and with an Introduction by* JULIET MCMASTER

352 pages | Colour plates, B&W drawings, maps, notes, bibliography,
    index
978-0-88864-437-4 | $39.95 paper
Biography | Art History

### Jane Austen & Company

*Collected Essays*
BRUCE STOVEL
NORA FOSTER STOVEL, *Editor*
JULIET MCMASTER, *Introduction*
ISOBEL GRUNDY, *Afterword*

978-0-88864-548-7 | $34.95 paper
978-0-88864-677-4 | $27.99 PDF
264 pages | Preface, introduction, afterword, bibliography
Literary Criticism | Jane Austen Studies